ANIMALS OF
AFRICA

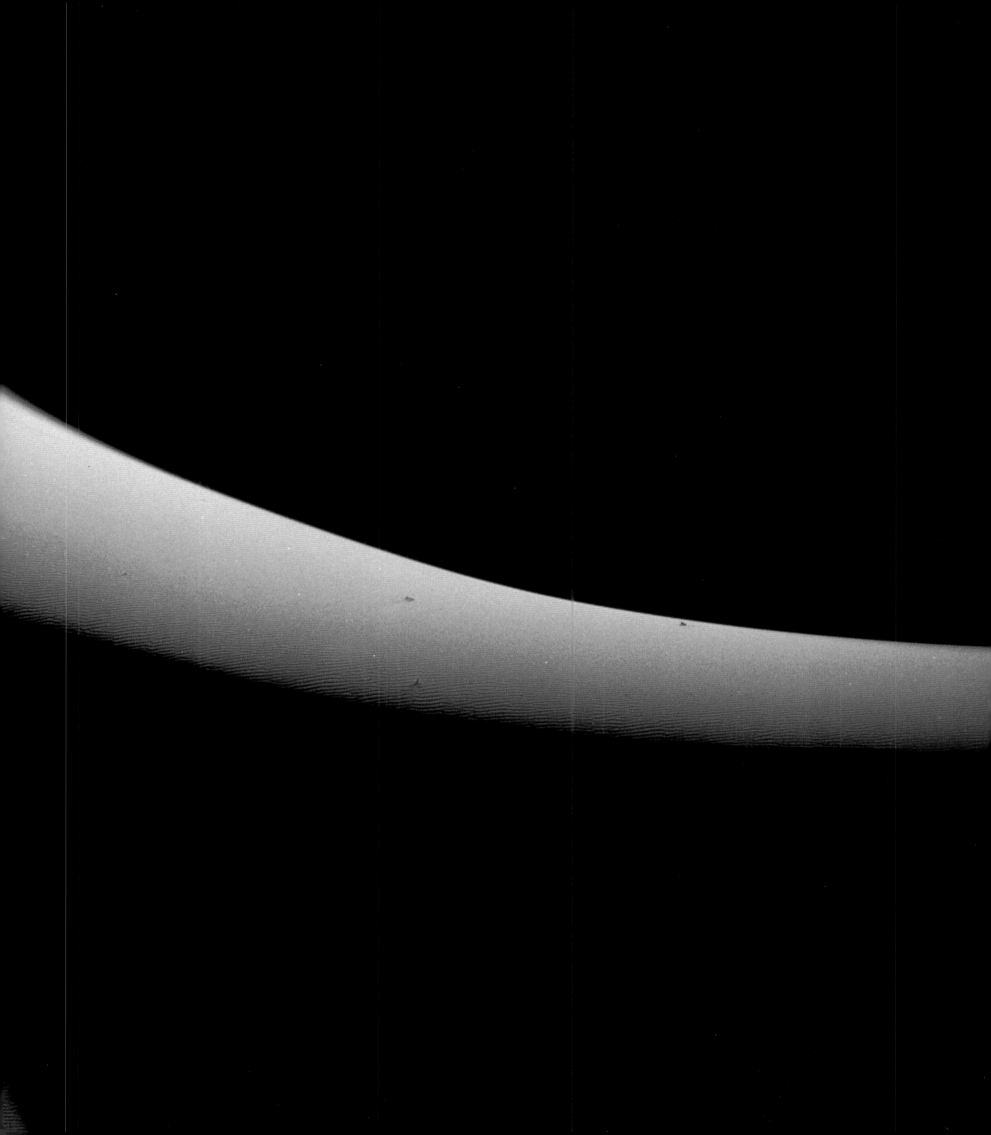

ANIMALS OF
AFRICA

THOMAS B. ALLEN

KÖNEMANN

Animals of Africa

PRODUCED BY
Charles O. Hyman, Visual Communications, Inc., Washington, D.C.

DESIGNED BY
Kevin Osborn, Research & Design, Ltd., Arlington, Virginia

PAGE 1
*Giraffes make an X,
marking their spot in
Botswana.*

PAGES 2-3
*Red-billed oxpeckers
hitchhike on a Cape
buffalo in Kenya.*

PAGES 4-5
*A bull elephant treads the
Kenya savanna. Mount
Kilimanjaro looms in the
background.*

PAGES 6-7
*Young lions cluster at a
water hole in the
Serengeti.*

PAGES 8-9
*A gemsbok stands amid
the dunes of the Namib
Desert in Namibia.*

PAGES 10-11
*A young mountain
gorilla peers from the
forest gloom in Rwanda.*

PAGES 12-13
*A horned impala buck
parades with his harem
in Kenya.*

ILLUSTRATIONS CREDITS
Abbreviations: (T) *top,* (B) *bottom,* (L) *left,* (R) *right*

JIM BRANDENBURG
8-9, 130(T), 132-133, 133(T), 139, 146-147, 172-173, 182(B), 182-183, 207

MITSUAKI IWAGO
4-5, 6-7, 22-23, 25, 28, 30-31, 34, 34-35, 36-37, 37, 38, 40-41, 41(T), 41(B), 42-43, 45(T), 45(B), 46(T),
46(B), 46-47, 48-49, 49(B), 50(T), 50(B), 50-51, 53, 54, 56-57, 58-59, 59, 60, 60-61, 62-63, 64, 65, 67, 68-69,
69(T), 69(B), 70, 71, 72(T), 72(B), 72-73, 74-75, 75(T), 75(B), 76-77, 80-81,
82-83, 90-91, 92(R), 93, 94, 94-95, 96-97, 99, 104, 105, 111, 112, 114(T), 114(B),
114-115, 116-117, 118-119, 119, 130(B), 130-131, 133(B), 134, 168(T), 168(B),
168-169, 170-171, 178, 182(T), 186, 196-197, 198-199, 216-217

FRANS LANTING
1, 12-13, 16, 21, 27, 32-33, 38-39, 44-45, 49(T), 79, 85, 87, 88, 92(L), 100, 102-103, 106-107, 108-109,
120-121, 122, 124, 126-127, 128-129, 134-135, 136-137, 141, 144-145, 146,
148-149, 150-151, 152-153, 153(T), 153(B), 154-155, 157, 158, 160-161, 162, 162-163,
165, 166, 177, 180-181, 181, 184-185, 185, 187, 188-189, 189, 190-191, 193, 195,
201, 202, 203, 204, 204-205, 211, 213, 217, 234-235, 237, 239, 240,
242-243, 244-245, 245, 246, 247, 250, 252

MICHAEL NICHOLS
10-11, 19, 142, 175, 208-209, 214, 219, 220, 220-221, 222-223,
224-225, 225, 226-227, 229, 230, 232, 233

SHIN YOSHINO
2-3

EARTH SATELLITE CORPORATION
249

Copyright © 1998 for this edition Könemann Verlagsgesellschaft mbH
Bonner Str. 126, D-50968 Köln

Production Manager: Detlev Schaper, Assistant: Nicola Leurs
Printing and Binding: Mateu Cromo Artes Gráficas S.A.
Printed in Spain

ISBN 3-8290-1086-9

10 9 8 7 6 5 4 3 2 1

THE PHOTOGRAPHERS

FRANS LANTING, a self-taught photographer and naturalist, was born in Rotterdam, Netherlands. In 1981, Frans drew international attention for a story about snow geese for *Geo* magazine, in collaboration with writer Barry Lopez.

In the last decade he has become a professional nomad, documenting wildlife and man's relationship with nature around the world. He has covered the migration of Monarch butterflies to Mexico, lived for months with albatrosses on small islands in the Pacific Ocean, spent a summer with Kwakiutl Indian artists carving masks from nature along Canada's west coast and camped among giant tortoises inside a volcano in the Galapagos Islands.

Since 1985, he has worked predominately with the *National Geographic* on challenging assignments such as searching for the last white rhinoceros in Zaire, circumnavigating under sail the remote South Georgia Island in the Antarctic, and being the first professional photographer to cover the fabled pygmy chimpanzee in the jungles of the Congo Basin.

In Madagascar he has documented wildlife and tribal traditions never photographed before. His pioneering coverage in the *National Geographic*, and dozens of other magazines, has done much to raise awareness worldwide about Madagascar's ecological problems.

MICHAEL "NICK" NICHOLS was born in Florence, Alabama in 1952. A pioneer in the use of flash mixed with ambient light, Nick's work is bound in energy, striving for photography with an edge. *Photo* magazine called him "The Indiana Jones of Photography," and the Overseas Press Club gave him a prize for reporting above and beyond the call of duty, an award usually reserved for combat photographers. Nick's work has been published in *National Geographic*, *Geo* and numerous other magazines. In 1988, Nick and Aperture Books produced *Gorilla, Struggle for Survival in the Virungas*, about the nearly extinct mountain gorilla living on the borders of Rwanda and Zaire. In 1996, World Press awarded him First Prize in the Nature and Environment category for *Wildlife in Ndoki, Central Africa*. His most recent book, *Keepers of the Kingdom*, is an in-depth photographic essay on the revolution in America's zoos, published by Thomasson-Grant & Lickle. In January 1996, he became a staff photographer for *National Geographic*, where he is presently photographing an essay on the endangered tiger.

MITSUAKI IWAGO was born in Tokyo in 1949, and has been taking pictures since childhood. After graduating, he made photography his career and soon gained recognition as one of the world's foremost wildlife and nature photographers. He has taken award-winning images in more than seventy countries, from the Galapagos Islands to the Serengeti Plain. From 1982 to 1984, he stayed with his family in Serengeti National Park, where he wrote and photographed his internationally-acclaimed, best-selling book, *Serengeti: Natural Order on the African Plain*. More recently he has published the spectacular books, *Mitsuaki Iwago's Whales* and *Mitsuaki Iwago's Kangaroos*. Mitsuaki's work has appeared in numerous books and magazines, including *National Geographic* and *Life*. In 1989, he began producing a video series, entitled *Mitsuaki Iwago's Nature World*, which he continues to do today in partnership with NHK Television.

JIM BRANDENBURG was born in Minnesota. He began his career as a natural history photographer and film maker while majoring in studio art at the University of Minnesota, Duluth. Jim became a contract photographer in 1978 for the *National Geographic*. He was twice named "Magazine Photographer of the Year" by the National Press Photographer's Association (NPPA). Jim was commissioned by the United States Postal Service to photograph and design a set of ten wildlife stamps, which were released on May 14, 1981. Among his award-winning books are *Brother Wolf—A Forgotten Promise*, *White Wolf—Living with an Arctic Legend*, and *Minnesota—Images of Home*. Jim's work has appeared in 16 *National Geographic* books and 17 *National Geographic* magazines. His national and international awards include the World Achievement Award from the United Nations Environmental Programme in Stockholm, Sweden. He serves on the board for the Defenders of Wildlife, the Friends of Boundary Waters Canoe Area, and the Wolf Ridge Environmental Learning Center. His work with wolves has been featured on all the major television networks, including ABC's *Prime Time Live*, and CBS's *Sunday Morning* with Charles Kuralt.

CONTENTS

A pattern of greater flamingos adorns Lake Makgadikgadi in Botswana.

AFRICA:
THE ENDANGERED ARK
BY JANE GOODALL

Louis S. B. Leakey, the man who introduced me to the study of chimpanzees, was a paleontologist, a discoverer of our roots. But he was also a man in love with Africa and its incomparable animals. He wrote, "This great wildlife population is, I believe, unmatched anywhere else on Earth. Incredible in its complexity, it evolved on a continent that for millions of years provided optimum conditions for life somewhere on its surface, even when undergoing volcanic upheavals and climatic changes and alterations of sea level. Because there was always some optimum area, the creatures of East Africa evolved with less natural disturbance than in many other places; and today they enjoy an almost unbelievable variety of habitats."

The variety still is there as Dr. Leakey knew it: mangrove swamps, open grasslands, rain forests, desert and near-desert, mountains that themselves encompass varying habitats on their slopes. And the animals are still there, particularly the ones he liked to call the giants—the elephants, the rhinos, the Cape buffalo and the hippos.

Dr. Leakey once told of the reaction that a visitor had after beholding animals from the porch of a game watchers' hotel. Spread out before the visitor were some 40 elephants and a herd of buffalo, all jostling for space. Now and then a baby sidled up to its elephant mother to nurse, or an elephant would squeal a warning if a buffalo came too close at the water hole. "It's *prehistoric!*" the watcher exclaimed.

Africa does indeed project a feeling of prehistory, a feeling that we have been there, that we have come from there. But that primeval image now is threatening to disappear, along with the wildlife that inhabits it. Africa's magnificent animals—the elephant, the rhino, the hippo, the gorilla, along with lesser known birds and mice and frogs—are disappearing because their forest habitat is being destroyed by the human population explosion. In addition, many animals are disappearing because, in some parts of Africa, they are hunted for the "bush meat" trade— chimpanzees, gorillas, and all kinds of endangered creatures are shot or trapped for food.

In the old days, the hunter would hunt for meat for his family and perhaps for the village. But today loggers are taking roads into the heart of the last remaining great rain forests of the African continent. With those roads comes opportunity for settlement along the sides of the roads. Hunters can go deeper and deeper into the forest. After they shoot the animals, they can put the bodies—dried usually in the sun or by smoke—onto the logging trucks for shipment into a town or settlement. So it is not just subsistence hunting anymore. It has become a business—making money by killing wild animals and selling them as food in the markets of parts of central and western Africa where bush meat is preferred over beef or goat or any other kind of domestic meat.

It was fortunate for me that Louis Leakey chose Tanzania for my chimpanzee study (it was Tanganyika when I began), for when independence came in 1981 there were strong wildlife protection laws in place. And politically Tanzania has been among the most—if not the most— stable of all the post-colonial era countries in Africa. Unfortunately, though, the economy grew gradually weaker, and it became ever more difficult to enforce wildlife laws. The poacher had much to gain—he was likely to get more money by killing an elephant and selling its tusks than he could expect to earn in ten years by legal means. For some, poaching became big business, and gangs were armed with sophisticated automatic weapons and new vehicles, while anti-poaching

In a gesture that is part of a "language more ancient than words," Jane Goodall greets a chimpanzee, closest genetic relative to humans. For more than 30 years she has observed the gregarious primates at Gombe Stream in Tanzania. In recent years her attention has turned to the survival in the wild and treatment in captivity of chimps and other primates.

patrols often had ancient cars with insufficient fuel and guns with little ammunition. And the same kind of thing happened in many other newly independent countries in Africa.

In order to preserve wild animal species it is, of course, necessary to preserve their habitat also. The tropical forest presents special problems: The fragile soils quickly lose fertility once the tree cover has gone; soil erosion sets in, especially where there is overgrazing of cattle and goats; crops become less and less productive. Gradually, where all was lush and green, the desert takes over. This spells doom for the wildlife—and for the peasants who have cut down the trees. They suffer crippling poverty and, in the struggle to survive from day to day, they cannot concern themselves with what will happen in the years ahead. Even when laws are passed to protect the rain forest, those laws are hard, if not impossible, to enforce. The only possible solution is to involve the local people in conservation efforts—to make it worth their while to cooperate. The Jane Goodall Institute, for example, is trying to boost local economies in areas where we operate—employing as many local villagers as possible, involving them in the projects, buying their produce. And in those places we have set up sanctuaries for orphaned chimpanzees, confiscated by government officials and handed over to us for care, we use them as ambassadors, as a focus for conservation education, teaching the local people, especially children, about the dangers of deforestation.

We use the sanctuaries also to teach the local children about these amazing relatives of ours, the chimpanzees. For the past 35 years we have been learning more and more about their similarities to ourselves. We know, for instance, that we differ from them genetically, in the composition of the DNA, by only just over one percent. There are similarities in the structure of the blood and the immune response system. And the anatomy of the chimpanzee's brain and central nervous system is more like ours than is that of any other living creature.

Most fascinating to me, are the incredible similarities in behavior—the long childhood, the importance of learning in an individual's life, the affectionate bonds that develop between family members and other individuals within a community. In their communication, chimpanzees show gestures that we see in human cultures around the world—kissing, embracing, holding hands, patting one another on the back, swaggering, tickling.

Chimpanzees can reason and solve simple problems, as demonstrated by their use of objects as tools for a variety of purposes in the wild. They can use and understand abstract symbols in their communication, as has been shown by language acquisition experiments. They are capable of tremendous memory feats. And all of us who have worked closely with chimpanzees, in natural or semi-natural situations, have absolutely no hesitation in affirming that they show emotions similar to—or perhaps identical to—those that we call joy, sorrow, fear, and despair.

I found that when I had my own child I could understand so well why a chimpanzee female when approached by others would seem to be fearful and threaten them away, because I felt the same. I felt rage when someone would seem to threaten my little baby, even if it was only waking him up when he was asleep.

The most important fact I learned was that chimpanzee mothers have fun with their kids. So I made time—half of every day, minimum—to be with my son. I also learned from the chimps that, until a child is capable of understanding the difference between right or wrong, you don't punish, you distract.

Once we are prepared to accept that human beings are not the only ones with personalities, we can gain a new respect, not only toward chimpanzees but also toward so many of the other amazing nonhuman beings with whom we share this planet. And nowhere are animals in danger more than in Africa.

Many people ask how anyone can care about chimpanzees and other non-human animals when there are so many human problems in Africa. We must understand that the human and nonhuman problems are linked. If the forest goes the wildlife goes, and eventually, the ever-increasing human population, no longer able to live in harmony with the natural world, will face starvation.

Is there, in fact, hope for Africa's future? Yes. Provided human populations develop programs that will stabilize, or optimize, their growth rate. It is very important to implement child health care programs along with family planning so that women can expect that their children will live—instead of knowing, as they do today, that many of them will die. There are many signs of hope. Along a lake shore in Tanzania, for example, villagers are planting trees where all the trees had disappeared. Women are taking more control over their lives, and once they become better educated, the birth rate then begins to drop. And the children are being taught about the terrible effects of habitual destruction.

Yes, there is hope. Especially if we can give hope to children, harness their energy, their concern. We must teach them how to care for the world around them so that societies, once again, can live in harmony with nature. And, if each one of us who cares about the future for our grandchildren, our great-grandchildren, does everything possible to save the world around us, those children of the future will be born into a world where they can still see blue sky, and trees, and hear the birds singing.

Sunrise mirrors an elephant in a pond in Botswana's Okavango Delta (opposite). The world's largest remaining herds of African elephants roam Botswana's wild lands.

THE HUNTERS

PAGES 22-23
Queen of beasts, a lioness blends into the tawny grass of the vast Serengeti Plain, heart of the African lion country and a gathering place for the predator's grazing prey. Here hunter and the hunted play their roles in an endless drama of survival.

A T CLOSE OF DAY on Tanzania's Serengeti Plain, when the lion's roar greets the dusk, the anthem of the wild—*hunt or behunted*—echoes through the mind. As night comes and the lions set out on the hunt, the eyes of hyenas pierce the darkness, seeking prey. A cheetah, invisible but emitting its scent, startles a herd of gazelles. They gallop off. There is a sudden, thrashing sound, and a new scent of death. *Hunt or be hunted.* A giraffe sniffs the air and moves closer to her newborn, vulnerable now but destined to grow and become too formidable for a single predator. *Hunt or be hunted.*

For many animals that hunt, night is the time they prowl and stalk. In the darkness, there is a fear. We know that because we feel it in the African night. Human consciousness was born in Africa, and we are not so far along that we do not sometimes feel within us the stirring of the predator, the fear of prey. But our emotions are not the emotions of, say, a lioness seeking food. She has no sense of cruelty, no feeling of pity. She is keeping herself and her cubs alive. She is in a struggle for life, a struggle that we can understand and admire, perhaps because there is still within us that ageless sense of the hunter. And perhaps there is envy when we gaze upon an animal so strong and fleet.

Animals do not seem to anticipate death. A gazelle or a zebra flees a predator not because it fears death but because it has seen or smelled something that has triggered its flight behavior. They flee not because they flee death but because they seek survival. One may fall prey to the hunter, but others will live on. Like the hunter, they are locked in a cycle of life and death.

Sometimes, when an animal dies, other members of the herd gather to watch at a distance. They seem to have a calmness about them, a sense that death is as inevitable as birth.

Eyes and ears on full alert, three cheetahs (opposite) scan the Serengeti. Each will hunt alone, stalking, then chasing prey at sprint speeds up to 70 miles per hour—so fast that few animals have a chance to escape.

LIONS

IN MYTHS and in heraldry, in adventurers' tales and children's stories, the lion reigns as the king of animal symbols, a model of savage beauty. Lions have so stirred the human imagination that scientists who first began studying animal behavior used the African lion (*Panthera leo*) as a subject. Their discoveries, while dispelling myths, also confirm some of the lore in old tales.

Take, for example, the concept of the "lion's share," which we all learned from the Aesop's fable. Looked at in terms of lion behavior, the fable turns out to be not far from wrong. Again and again lions have been observed moving in on prey killed by another lion or, more often, by lionesses. A lion will snarl and strike out with his paws as he wrests away a large portion—as much as 80 pounds of meat or more at a kill. Often, however, males will guard their portion, keeping lionesses away from it—and then share it with cubs.

Most lions of the African savanna live in groups called prides. Each of these complex societies consists of two or more adult males and several females and juveniles. The territory of each pride is several miles in diameter, with boundaries that overlap into the adjacent territories. Prides generally stay intact as long as the food supply is abundant. The females in a pride most often are related, with sisters, cousins, mothers, and daughters all working together in the group. The cubs of one mother are adopted by other mothers. In a kind of day-care arrangement, mothers share the suckling and the guarding of a pride's cubs. While some mothers and maturing cubs are on the hunt, other mothers and cubs stay in the heartland of the pride's territory and keep watch over the pride's youngest members. Cubs need protection from adult males. To them, an unprotected cub is prey.

The gestation period for lions is 108 days on average, an extremely short time for such a large animal. The result is that newborn cubs are usually very small—about a pound in weight and about a foot long—and immature. Blind at birth, they do not have full sight for two weeks or so. The cubs remain close to the adult females, and enjoy maternal affection and protection during the most vulnerable stage of their early life. Small and infrequent litters make it possible for a lioness to spend a great deal of time with her cubs, even after they have been weaned.

Cubs nurse for about six to eight months, and depend upon adults for all of their food until they are about two years old. Weaning begins about three months after birth, when the cubs begin to eat meat. Young cubs learn by watching the adults, and by playing to perfect their hunting skills. They are never far from their mother or her female kin until they are about six months old. Then they begin to tag along behind the hunters, learning the elements of hunting and the harsh etiquette of the kill. By the time they are one and a half years old they are hunting with the pride and claiming their share of the fallen prey.

Most pride lionesses remain in the pride for life. Inevitably, the males leave, as do some lionesses. They become nomads, living without the protective society of the pride. These occasional defections keep the pride's size in proportion to the food available.

Lions prosper during the rainy season, from November through May, when the Serengeti is green and dappled with sparkling lakes. Prey is abundant then. But during the rest of the year, when the plain can look like a desert, prey is scarce, and lions must hunt for stragglers or smaller animals of the woods. Lions may go for a week or more without food. In a pride desperate for food, adults will eat even while cubs starve to death.

The pride accommodates to a rhythm of abundance and scarcity by having a relatively loose social structure and by staking out a territory and defending it. A pride, which may include 30 or more lions, does not have a ruling lion or lioness. The lack of a hierarchy means that the meting out of food is not determined by rank, especially when there is a shortage of food. In the hierarchy of other animal societies, subordinate animals would

A six-year-old lion, king of the beasts, prowls his African domain in northern Botswana. His thick mane protects his neck during fights with other males.

A cub, learning to be a lion, imitates the staring, ears-up posture of its mother. The lessons will continue until the cub is one and a half years old and ready to hunt with the pride.

cower before the dominant. In the lion society, some may be weak and others strong, but the weak still can fight for food.

The social structure also allows for cooperative hunting. Sometimes pride members go off to hunt in pairs; other times, when the hunt demands it, they can stalk on a broad front. They prefer to hunt large animals—wildebeests, buffalo, zebras, wild hogs, giraffes, impalas, and other antelope—but they will eat anything they can catch, killing small prey with a swipe of the claw. They hunt inside their own territory, which can range in size up to 150 square miles, according to the density of prey. Territoriality aids lionesses, giving them a permanent living space full of familiar places for hiding cubs and seeking prey

The pride's males mark its boundaries by roaring or by spraying the brush with strong-smelling urine. Nomadic lions, unwelcome visitors to territories, can tell by a sniff how recently a territorial male passed on patrol— and thus how safe it would be to stroll through the territory.

Nomadic males begin their wandering at around the age of three and a half, when they are expelled from the pride by dominant males. Sometimes two or three brothers, expelled at the same time, will become nomads together, following migratory herds of zebras or wildebeests. As a nomad, the young male matures, growing in strength and prowess until he can challenge a pride male. Usually, the challenge consists of fierce snarls and flailing claws, with little or no bloodshed. Sometimes the challenge escalates to a fight to the death. Wounded lions may recover but, hobbled or sickly, they risk an early death when they become prey for hyenas. (Lions in the wild live eight to ten years; in captivity they may live 25 years or more.) When a nomad succeeds in entering a pride, its females accept the newcomer, thereby welcoming new genes to the pride.

Members of prides can count on family help if they are wounded. One young lioness, wounded in one leg and unable to hunt for nearly nine months, lived on meat brought to her by other members of the pride.

In most prides, lionesses do 80 to 90 percent of the hunting. On a typical hunt involving several members of the pride, slinking females pad ahead, stalking prey. The males lope along in the rear, and to the untrained eye, the males seem to be letting the females do the work. But, on the hunt with the lionesses, the males do have a role: They protect the cubs that stumble along far behind their mothers and other female relatives. When the lionesses make a kill and the males move in to get their lion's share, they guarantee food for cubs that cannot depend on mother's generosity. Mothers have been seen driving their cubs away from a kill. Cubs that manage to snatch away a morsel often have to give it up under assault from mother.

Lions must especially hunt together when the prey are large animals, such as zebras, which are too strong and wily for a lone lion to pull down and kill. Against a concerted assault by large prides, however, zebras cannot prevail. In a study of lion hunts, zebras were particularly vulnerable, with 1,300 kills recorded in 4,750 hunts. During the same period, lions stalked giraffes 200 times and were successful only six times. Besides the usual diet of impalas and tsessebe antelope, lion prey include young elephants, Cape buffalo, and hippopotamuses.

Lions devote little time to hunting, usually spending about 20 hours a day sleeping or lying around. Usually, though, they keep their eyes on the sky, for the sight of vultures circling down on a carcass will launch a lion even in the heat of midday. Lions are opportunistic, and carrion is easy food

When lions hunt, they rely as much on timing as on their retractile claws and long canine teeth. They watch for that single moment when their quarry slackens its vigil, or, on the run, slackens its speed. By reacting one moment too late, the hunted gives the hunter that instant that lies between life and death, between hunger and the lion's share.

PAGES 30-31
Lion and lioness share a kopje, a rock outcropping on the Serengeti. They are probably a breeding pair, for adult male and female are rarely together for any other reason. Mating may occur at any time, but usually the females in a pride tend to give birth about the same time of year.

PAGES 32-33
Two lionesses work together as they stalk prey. One of their strategies: Approach the prey from two sides so that if one lioness misses, the other will seize the victim as it flees. Sometimes members of a pride fan out and then close in on a quarry from all sides.

*A lioness (above) sharpens her weapons. Lions can
retract their claws to keep them from getting blunt.
Sharp and deeply curved, their design is perfect for
the job of grasping and holding prey. Hairy ankles
and toes help muffle the lion's stealthy tread.*

*Galloping across a Serengeti grassland, a zebra tries to
outrun a lioness (opposite). Lions and lionesses usually
give up the chase if a sprint after prey lasts more than
100 yards. They will eat anything they can catch, but a
hunt for big animals is the best investment of energy.
A zebra carcass could feed a pride for three days.*

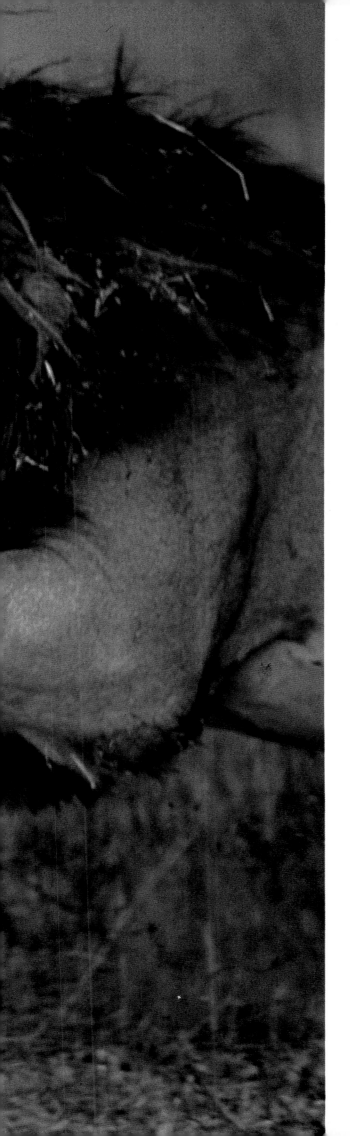

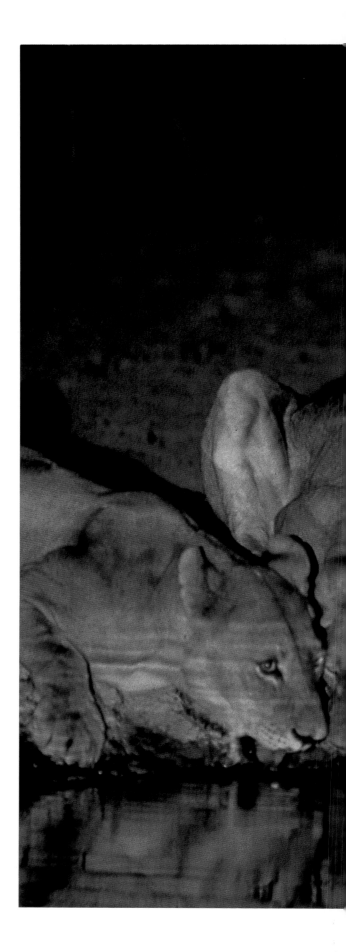

*Opportunistic lionesses, drawn to a dead elephant, give
up the night's hunt for a chance to dig into carrion
(above). Lions once were believed to disdain carrion,
leaving it to the hyenas. Modern research reveals
that lions will scavenge, that hyenas will hunt,
and that each will steal the other's kills.*

*Lionesses line up for water (opposite). They keep watch
over water holes, magnets for prey and predators.
Observers have suggested that in some areas a water
hole can be neutral ground, where kills are rare.
But vigilance probably keeps down the toll.*

*A lion (above) spends most of his time lying around.
Lionesses and cubs (top) also do little during the day,
but a mother cannot keep her eyes off her cubs, which
are vulnerable until they are too big and too
skilled for hyenas or jackals to catch and kill.*

*Two young males, old enough to have been driven
from their birth prides, meet at a dried-up water
hole in the Serengeti (opposite).*

PAGES 42-43
*As a storm approaches on the Serengeti, members of a
pride take catnaps. They display a copycat custom of
social animals: What one does, others also do.*

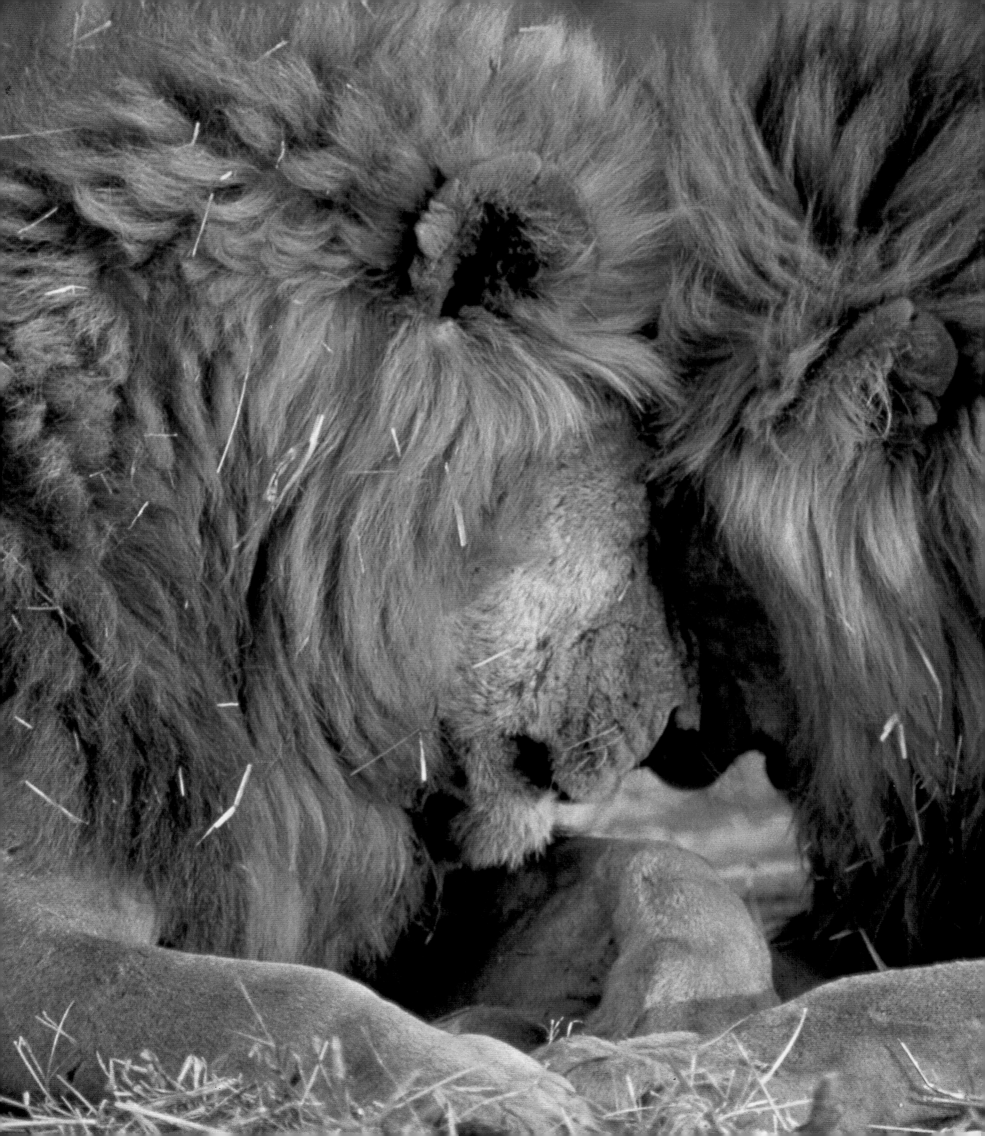

*Head to head and mane to mane, two males (opposite)
confront but do not duel. Two other males (top) square
off for combat in a fight triggered by a newcomer's
invasion of a pride's territory. His skull pierced by
a fatal bite (above), the invader dies—a rare
ending for a ritual that usually consists
of roars and swipes of claws.*

*A roaring male approaches a sexually aroused female
(top) and then mates with her (above). The sexual
union ends abruptly (opposite) in a flurry of clouts
and threats. The male refrains from biting the
female because neither he nor she intends
to fight. In moments, both will rest.*

*Lionesses raise cubs on their own as single parents
(opposite). But lionesses of the pride—united by
kinship—share in cub care. A mother flanked by two
cubs (top) may be watching her own and others' cubs.*

*The devoted care that mothers give cubs (above) goes on
for about a year and a half. Cubs depend upon the
pride for food until they are at least 16 months old.
By then, the mother may be about to give birth
to another litter of two to four cubs.*

*Rough and tumble play (top) prepares cubs for the adult
world. Sometimes the fighting looks real (above), but
teeth are not bared and the awkward stances do not
deliver the power of adult battling. This cub may
seem to be alone (opposite), but mothers
rarely let cubs stray out of sight.*

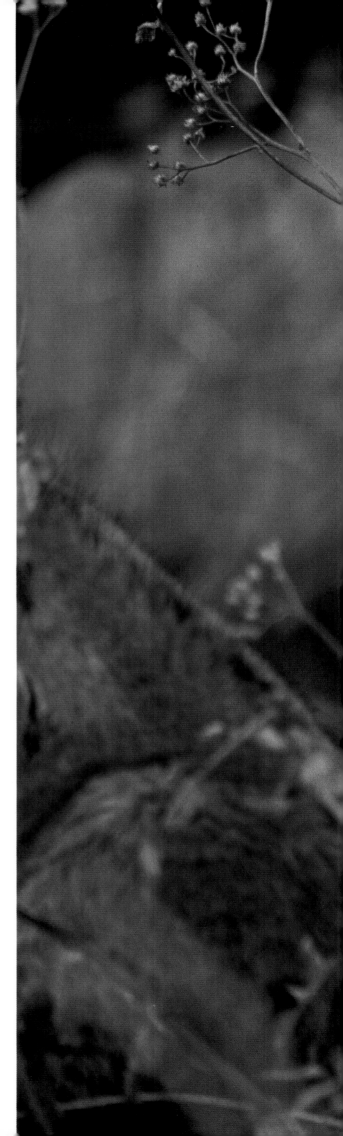

CHEETAHS

CHEETAHS, the world's fastest land animals, barely seem to touch the ground when they streak across the grasslands in pursuit of prey. The cheetah (*Acinonyx jubatus*) gets up to speed through a combination of running and leaping. Going into a sprint, the light-boned cheetah uses every inch of its long, lithe body to accelerate from 0 to 45 miles per hour in two seconds. Its nonretractable claws and wide paw pads provide traction. Its large nostrils and lungs enable it to produce tremendous bursts of oxygen. Its leg muscles are complex; one set is designed for walking, the other for high-speed hunts.

Slowed down, the cheetah's sprint looks like this: Pushes off on one of its powerful back legs, sending the body forward. Launches off the ground with the other back leg. Touches the ground with one front leg. Touches down the other front leg, which then pulls the cheetah forward. The spine acts like a spring, fully flexing the body. (A race horse, by comparison, keeps its spine rigid and relies entirely on its legs for speed.) In the air, the flying cheetah moves so fast that it uses its tail as a rudder.

Such speed demands a short, enormous surge of energy. The cheetah's highest recorded speed, 71 miles per hour, can be sustained for about 300 yards. On its hunts, the cheetah is well aware of the limits of its built-for-speed body. Most other cats hunt at night and ambush their prey. Cheetahs will hunt at night, but they are frequently seen hunting in the early morning or late afternoon. A cheetah stalks its prey until only about 50 yards separate the hunter and the hunted. At this point the cheetah charges, its elongated eyes giving it a wide-angle view as the prey tries to evade with tight turns. Lions give up the chase after 100 yards or so, but cheetahs can run more than three miles—at an average speeds of 45 miles per hour. The hunt may end in a sprint that lasts from 20 to 60 seconds.

When the cheetah overtakes its prey, it smashes into the animal, knocking it down. It then grabs the prey's throat and closes its jaw on the victim's windpipe, suffocating it. To thwart lion hijackers, the cheetah often hauls its meal into trees. (Lions can leap into trees, but usually do not climb them.) Cheetahs use trees, termite mounds, and hilltops as vantage points, keen eyes ever searching for prey. Cheetahs, which exhaust themselves in their sprint chases, seem to work harder for their food than most other big cats.

The cheetah's hunting success varies with terrain and prey. But usually it can make only one charging sprint in a chase. Then it must get its breath, perhaps losing the prey. Few animals, however, can escape the cheetah. Usually a prey's only chance is to spot the cheetah early or elude an inexperienced cheetah cub.

Mothers with cubs may make a kill every day; other adults hunt every two to five days. Cubs—usually three, though there may be as many as eight in a litter—begin to follow the hunt when they are about six weeks old. At the age of six months, they start learning about hunting from their mother. She will, for instance, capture a small mammal and then present it to her cubs alive. Under her gaze, they then can practice the usual cheetah killing technique: Seize the prey by the throat and strangle it. The cubs may spend as long as two years with their mother before going off on their own.

The cheetah's prey includes gazelles, springbok, steenbok, duikers, and impalas, along with birds, hares, and the young of warthogs, kudu, hartebeests, oryx, roans, and sables. The primary food for most cheetah populations are small species of antelope, particularly impalas and Thomson's gazelles. Bird-catching cheetahs have been credited with luring the prey by imitating a targeted bird's call. Perhaps, the cheetah does have a relatively muted repertoire that includes growling, hissing, barking, purring, loud yelping that can be heard a mile away, and a chirping sound that mothers use to call to their cubs.

At maturity, the cheetah has yellow or tan fur with solid black spots that cover nearly all of the body, except the throat, which is white. The long, spotted tail ends in a series of black

The world's fastest land mammal speeds across the Serengeti Plain (opposite). The cheetah's supple spine allows legs to tuck in a powerful thrust.

rings and a white tip. Its head seems too small for its body, but the proportion fits into the design for speed. The cheetah's distinctive teardrop markings camouflage it in shadowy grass. The dark outlines around its eyes help to shade them against the African sun. In maturity, cheetahs weigh from 110 to 130 pounds, stand about 32 inches tall at the shoulder, and are about 56 inches long; their tails, which have a rudder-like upward curve, are 30 to 32 inches long.

The cheetah family arrangement differs considerably from the lion pride. Females usually live solitary lives, except when they have cubs; but they will remain in the territory of their own birth. Males travel in "coalitions" of two to four, defending territories against other males. Males are believed to maintain their coalitions for life. Their territories encompass the territories of females, but male and female get together only to mate.

"Cheetah" comes from a Hindi word that translates as "spotted one." The spotted ones once had a vast domain, stretching from biblical lands and the Arabian Peninsula through parts of Russia and India and much of Africa. Tamed by Sumerians and worshipped by Egyptians, cheetahs became pets in many Asian courts, as noted by Marco Polo. Famous cheetah pet owners include Charlemagne, Genghis Khan, and Akbar the Great of India who, in the second half of the sixteenth century, reportedly kept 9,000 cheetahs! Asians began the practice of using cheetahs as hunters.

Known as "hunting leopards," trained cheetahs would be taken, hooded and on horseback or in a cart, to a likely spot for what was called "coursing," or hunting by sight, rather than by scent. The hunter would sight game, remove the hood, and unleash the cheetah. Like a falcon, the cheetah would pull down the game, and its master would claim it. The cheetah got a share of the kill as a reward.

Cheetah pelts were cherished as symbols of power, but the killing of cheetahs for pelt or sport did not imperil the species until modern times. At the turn of the nineteenth century

there were about 100,000 cheetahs on earth in a range that included India. (The cheetahs in India had been wiped out by the 1950s.) Today cheetahs are extremely endangered, with only about 12,500 alive in Africa. Namibia, with an estimated 2,500, has the largest population. Because there is only one cheetah species in Africa, the cats are particularly vulnerable to epidemics and are considered at high risk for extinction.

Africa's leopard (*Panthera pardus*), whose populations include several subspecies, is not as imperiled. Hundreds of thousands live in sub-Saharan Africa, although farmers and poachers exterminated them in South Africa. They can adapt to habitats ranging from the desert to 18,500 feet up the slope of Mount Kilimanjaro, a fact used by Hemingway in his classic short story, "The Snows of Kilimanjaro." Leopards spend much of their time in trees, where, sometimes spending days at a leisurely feast, they eat without fear of meat-snatching lions. During a drought or a shortage of large prey, leopards will eat insects and birds and even catch fish. A night-hunter known as "companion of the moon," the leopard may range over 15 to 20 miles in search of food.

Africa is home to some 20 small cats, such as the caracal (*Felis caracal*) and the serval (*F. serval*), and catlike animals, such as the African civet (*Civettictis civetta*). They are all secretive, cunning, and rarely seen except in zoos. "After 18 years in Africa, I have seen a serval twice, a civet once, and the rest not at all," wrote naturalist Norman Myers. "But I have come across lions and cheetahs hundreds of times."

The serval, a sharp-eared, solitary night hunter, has been known to leap nearly ten feet into the air to snare an unsuspecting bird. The caracal, a supple predator of woodland and savanna, is about the size of a house cat. It too can leap into the air to catch birds and can pull down a dik-dik as big as itself. The civet, about the size of a cocker spaniel, eats small mammals, snakes, frogs, and insects. It also prowls around villages at night in search of chickens and goat kids.

Fierce as its threat posture may look (opposite), the cheetah is easily tamed. Indian princes used them to hunt gazelles. Black tear-drop markings around the cheetah's eyes cut down sun glare.

PAGES 56-57
As the sun sets over the Serengeti, a cheetah climbs an acacia tree, a frequent roost for the climbing cat.

Cheetahs (opposite) monitor scent and sound while planning the next move to the next meal. Hidden in grass, cheetahs flick their black-banded ears to pick up movement by potential prey. Prey watch for that black spot in the grass.

Even as cubs (above), cheetahs show family traits: eyes watchful, ears on high alert.

*A cheetah, its long tail acting like a rudder (above),
overtakes a Thomson's gazelle. Two cheetahs share
another Tommie kill (opposite). A study of cheetah
hunts showed that seven out of 12 kills
were Thomson's gazelles.*

PAGES 62-63
*Lone hunter of the Serengeti, a cheetah pauses atop a
kopje, high ground for predators seeking prey
and for prey on watch for predators.*

On the prowl (above) or between hunts (opposite),
cheetahs live in small groups—a female with cubs
and a "coalition" of males. Like house cats,
cheetahs purr and lick each other in a form
of affectionate communication.

HYENAS

YENAS have two niches in Africa. As real animals, filling the night with their maniacal whoops and laughs, they hunt aggressively and are confident enough to terrorize lions. As creatures of myth, over the centuries they have generated fantastic tales of depravity and horror. Until modern times, reality and myth so commingled that the hyena ranked as the most misunderstood and most maligned animal in Africa.

The truth about the hyena began to emerge in the 1970s out of the observations of such pioneers in animal behavior studies as Jane Goodall, Hugo Van Lawick, George B. Schaller, and Hans Kruuk. What they saw dispelled the basic myth that hyenas were only scavengers. The researchers saw hyenas and lions compete as hunters, and often steal each other's kills, with hyenas often driving lions away from their own kills. Hyenas, however, are not greedy; they take away only what they need.

In Botswana's Chobe National Park, hyena clans, sometimes numbering as many as 40, have confronted lion prides, not to compete over food but to fight. Lions, in what appeared to be an attempt to rid their territory of hyenas, attacked the rivals. The lions killed—but did not eat—the hyenas. Lionesses sought the dominant female hyena.

The family Hyaenidae encompasses four species: the spotted, the brown, the striped, and the aardwolf, which eats termites and insect larvae. The most intensively studied is the spotted hyena (*Crocuta crocuta*), which ranges in length from 35 to 64 inches and weighs about 88 pounds, with females usually longer and heavier than males. Spotted hyenas roam savannas, desert, and mountainsides either as hunters, running down their prey like wolves, or as scavengers, feasting on carrion. Hyenas can go for several days without water. Their incredibly strong jaws and digestive tracts can dispose of entire corpses, including bones, hide, and hair. A hyena can consume up to one-third of its body weight in one feeding frenzy.

Spotted hyenas hunt in packs, typically chasing a herd of migrating wildebeests until a weak or young one falters, then pouncing on it and consuming it on the spot. A chase may go on for a mile or more, with hyenas achieving speeds of 25 to 30 miles per hour. Around a kill, hyenas vocalize, their giggling and growling inspiring the tag "laughing hyenas."

As many as 80 hyenas live together in large clans, which divide into packs. At the core of the clan is a group of related females born into the clan and forming a hierarchy. The top-ranking female mates only with the ranking member of the male hierarchy. Many males, at sexual maturity, wander off to join another clan.

Cubs—there are usually one or two in a litter—are ferocious. Born with eyes open and a mouthful of teeth, they fight savagely, sometimes from the moment of birth. It is not unheard of for the first two cubs in a litter to fight while their mother is licking a third one dry. Such fighting kills as many as one out of every four cubs before adulthood. The fiercest fighting often is between two sisters. The stronger sister will kill the weaker, beginning a struggle that will take her into the competition for ruling the female hierarchy.

Clans stake out large territories, which members mark off by depositing a pasty, extremely smelly secretion on grass and bushes. They greet and identify each other in ceremonies that resemble the greetings of dogs (although hyenas are not related to dogs). A hyena usually will not eat a dead member of its own clan, but it will eat rotting crocodiles or dead cheetahs during lean periods.

Myths about hyenas originated from confusion about their sexual activity. Male and female mate just as other mammals do, but male and female genitalia are quite similar in appearance. One theory holds that the female has a large amount of male hormones to increase her aggressiveness. Whatever the biological reason, the confusion inspired claims that hyenas could change sex at will. This notion led to accusations of witchcraft and the belief that witches can turn themselves into hyenas. And there was also the chilling fact that hyenas could make a corpse—including a human one—disappear.

Predator and prey seem to mutually ignore each other as a spotted hyena trots past a flock of flamingoes. Some observers believe that animals do not react to a predator's profile but flee when the predator turns and the profile becomes a head-on image.

Spotted hyenas mob the carcass of a wildebeest calf
(opposite), captured and killed by a pack, part of a large
clan. Feeding etiquette may look crude (above), but
etiquette based on rank within the clan hierarchy
determines which animals have the right to
take choice parts of a kill (top).

*Keeping in touch, members of a hyena clan recognize
each other by sight and scent (above). They mark
off boundaries of the clan territory with scent
from specialized glands. In any group,
females dominate males, usually
without any fighting.*

*Rank has its privileges in a hyena clan, where only the
leading male in the hierarchy can mate (above). The
clan, with male and female hierarchies, is built around
related females that remain in their birth clan;
males may move from one clan to another.*

Night hunters that cause nightmares by day, hyenas
became the subjects of myths inspired by faces that
look devilish (above) and howling that sounds
fiendish (opposite). People have killed them
as harbingers of evil; others have given
them tribal dead to eat.

A roll in the mud (top) cools off a hyena, which
juts a jaw that is the most powerful, in proportion
to size, of any mammal. Specialized teeth
and a formidable digestive system enable
it to crush and consume bones.

Whether getting a face washing (above) or playing at fighting (top), hyena cubs get attentive mothering. In a pack of hyenas (opposite), male and female are difficult to tell apart except by comparison: Females are bigger.

PAGES 76-77
Lionesses gang up to attack a lone hyena, killing it not for food but because they seem to hate it. Hyenas have also been seen making unprovoked attacks on lions.

WILD DOGS

PAGES 80-81
Wild dogs chase a doomed wildebeest. Cooperating in a hunt, the predators charge into a wildebeest herd, then cut out an ill or injured beast as an easy victim.

THE WILD DOG (*Lycaon pictus*), although a social animal like a lion or hyena, is also a nomad. Traveling across grassland, savanna, and open woodland, packs of five to 30 wild dogs hunt in one area for a while and then move on. The wild dog, also known as the African hunting dog and "the painted wolf," does not seem to be territorial. When the ranges of packs overlap, there does not appear to be any trouble among neighbors. During large migrations of potential prey, the packs merge, with hundreds of dogs gathering, in apparent harmony, to share in the bounty.

The dogs usually hunt in packs, especially to attack and slay large mammals. Some packs specialize in pulling down zebras. Dogs will also hunt on their own, going after rodents, hares, or other small creatures. Dogs have also been seen storing meat in holes in the ground, which serve as pantries on days when the hunt is unsuccessful.

Teamwork helps not only to pull down a 550-pound zebra but also to raise young. There may be as many as 16 pups in a litter, and to take care of them, the nomads stay in one place. The pup den—usually an abandoned aardvark hole—becomes the hub of pack activity. Males and females share in the care of the pups, and some adults stay behind on guard duty when the pack goes off to hunt.

Watching a hunt begin near a den full of wild dog pups, research scientist George Schaller noted that the dogs "exuberantly play and push their muzzles into the corners of each other's mouths—a greeting display derived from the food-begging behavior of pups. The activity probably gets the hunters in the right mood for a communal endeavor—just as a pep rally does for us."

A pack on the hunt can maintain a speed of more than 40 miles per hour for nearly 3.5 miles, whooping and wailing to keep in touch with each other. Like other predators, the wild dogs do not always get their prey. Their success rate is relatively low; typically, one chase out of three ends in a kill.

At a kill, the dogs crowd around and bolt their food, but without the snarling, nasty behavior that lions display. And they share. An injured dog arriving at a kill too late to get any food might get dinner when one of his pack mates regurgitates a piece of meat for him. Or a dog may be allowed to eat at kills without having participated in the capture of the prey.

Back at the den, the dogs regurgitate meat as meal donations for the pups and the dogs left to guard them. At age three months, when the pups are old enough to go on a kill, they are allowed to eat first. Hungry adults, including the dominant ones, often allow young dogs to eat their fill before the adults eat the leftovers, if there are any. Low-ranking members of the hierarchy, especially males, help to protect and feed pups old enough to eat solid food.

On average, there are about ten animals in a pack, with adult males usually outnumbering adult females two to one. Some packs have as many as eight adult males and only one adult female. Sexually mature sisters, eight months to two years old, will almost always leave their birth pack and join one that does not have sexually mature females. Eventually, one of the sisters will emerge as the dominant female in the new pack. At that point, her sisters will leave to find another pack. Over time, about half of the males also drift away, usually as bands of brothers.

In a typical pack there are several related males and several females, usually related to each other—but not to any of the males. The females have their own hierarchy, as do the males. Almost always, only the dominant male and the dominant female breed. They also generally are strong enough to prevent lower-ranking males and females from mating.

The struggle for dominance is fiercest among the females. After a savage fight, one of the dueling females will slink out of the pack, her fate almost certain death because of her wounds and her banishment from the protection of the pack.

Wild dogs once were found throughout sub-Saharan Africa. Now there are only believed to be 4,000 to 5,000. This presents researchers with a mystery: Why are these carnivores so rare, compared to lions and hyenas?

Wild dogs head out for a night hunt in Botswana (opposite). They can keep food undigested for hours so that when they return they can feed non-hunting kin with regurgitated meat.

THE GRAZERS

THE GRAZERS—giraffes, zebras, wildebeests, antelope—spend much of their time finding vegetation and eating it. Canny, swift, and resourceful, the grazers have these traits because upon them depends the balance between those that kill and those that are killed.

Ecologists call the grazers the "herbivore guild," animals of various species that share a grazing area. While wildebeests are feeding on grass, giraffes are nibbling on trees. Zebras, wildebeests, and topis all eat red oat grass, but at different times, following the growth cycle of the grass.

Grazers live in herds, protecting themselves by sheer numbers. On East Africa's great Serengeti Plain, where grazers gather by the millions, there are more animals assembled in one place than anywhere else on earth. Herds protect local populations and ultimately the species itself. But survival finally gets down to a matter of one animal living or dying, and that single animal, pursued by a predator, trying to survive by running for its life. Relying on speed or evasive tactics, it does its part to preserve its species.

Grazers usually are migrants, moving from place to place in search of green grass and water. When the dry season comes to the Serengeti Plain, for example, 1.5 million wildebeests and 200,000 zebras migrate more than 800 miles to the west and north to the open woodlands and the rich pastureland of Kenya's Masai Mara National Game Reserve. From around May to November they will stay there. Then, as the rains green the Serengeti once more, they return.

Camouflage helps to keep grazers alive. Stripes and spots break up the shape of an antelope's body, simulating streaks of sunlight to confuse the hunter. A zebra, conspicuous by day, blends into the darkness of night, when the lion is more likely to hunt.

PAGES 82-83
Thousands of migrating wildebeests and a few zebras weave a pattern of survival on the Serengeti Plain. Zebras get the choice spot under an acacia tree, along with dominant wildebeests. Predators pick off the weak and the unlucky beyond this inner circle.

An impala doe (opposite) chews her cud on a Botswana grassland. During rainy seasons she belongs to a grazing group of females and young, separate from male groups, distinguished by their horns.

GIRAFFES

THE TALL and silent giraffe has awed people since prehistoric times. In cave paintings dating to the era of a green Sahara, this strange, long-necked creature, which is found only in Africa, appears frequently. The giraffe did not make its formal debut in Britain until 1827 when Mohamed Ali, Pasha of Egypt, presented one as a diplomatic gift. Its scientific name, *Giraffa camelopardalis*, recalls the confusion that the animal caused when Europeans first beheld this "camel-leopard," a name that persisted for many years. Myth makes giraffes mute. Actually, though quiet, these lordly animals grunt, snort, and bleat. Mothers make a whistling call to their young, which may bleat in return.

The world's tallest mammal, the male giraffe towers 17 feet from toe to top of head and weighs on average about 1,760 pounds; females are slightly shorter and lighter. (The record height for a male is 19 feet.) A giraffe's body is relatively small, compared to its long neck and knobby-kneed legs, which can propel the animal at speeds up to 35 miles per hour. It earned its name from an Arabic word that means "one who walks swiftly," and its walk is as stately as it is swift. The two left legs move forward at the same time, then the right legs. With each stride, its great neck swings about widely and rhythmically, "like something in a dream," an observer once wrote. When a giraffe suddenly starts to gallop, its forelegs hurl it forward. The forelegs and hind legs then come together as the neck arches in a graceful forward motion. Because of the gait, the legs appear to differ greatly in size; in fact, the forelegs are only a slight bit longer than the hind legs.

Human beings, like most mammals, have seven neck vertebrae. So do giraffes, though their neck vertebrae are elongated to eight inches or more in length. Strung together, they create the long, flexible neck. Much about the giraffe's body is strange, from its double-hoofed feet to what seem to be horns. These are actually bony masses covered with skin and tufts of hair. At birth, these "ossicones" are cartilaginous knobs. They then rapidly turn into bone, forming two to four horns. Because giraffes are closely related to deer, some scientists believe that the ossicones may be relicts of pedicles at a time when ancestors had antlers.

The giraffe has extremely high blood pressure, about two or three times the blood pressure of a healthy human. The pressure is needed to pump blood 10 to 12 feet up the carotid artery from its 25-pound heart to its brain. Gravity helps to lower the pressure as the blood nears the brain; otherwise, the surge of high-pressure blood would damage the brain. When a giraffe bends down, valves prevent blood from rushing to the head. At the same time, a net of tissue below the brain is temporarily engorged, keeping excess blood from flowing to the brain. When the giraffe straightens up, the valves open and the excess blood resumes its course to the heart. Without such a system, the giraffe could not survive.

Found in open woodland and wooded grassland throughout sub-Saharan Africa, giraffes are still common in eastern and southern Africa, but poaching has cut down their numbers in the west. Once there were 100 or more in a herd, but now a herd may number only two to ten animals.

The giraffe lives on what it can browse, plucking leaves with its 17-inch tongue or pulling a branch into its mouth and pulling off leaves with a twist of its head. It prefers the leaves of the acacia trees, which are also known as giraffe trees or African camel's thorn. But there are more than 100 plant species on the giraffe's menu, including flowers, vines, herbs, along with an occasional weaver-bird nest. If there are chicks in the nest, the giraffe eats them too, gaining some extra minerals from their bones. Giraffes also get minerals by gnawing on the bones of animals killed and left by hyenas and other predators.

Males tend to stretch higher for food than females, lessening the feeding competition between them. The typical feeding stance for males is a full vertical stretch up to the leaves. A female giraffe usually feeds by curling her

A giraffe trio marches across an East African grassland (opposite). On the run, a giraffe strides swiftly, swinging its neck from side to side as it moves its two left legs forward at the same time, then both right legs.

Long legs outspread in an awkward bow, a giraffe sucks up water. Special valves in the giraffe's jugular and a network of tiny veins keep high-pressure blood from rushing to the brain when a giraffe bends down for a drink.

neck to nibble on lower trees and shrubs.

Thorns do not bother these ruminants. The tongue is tough and muscular, and thick, gluey saliva helps to ease thorns down the long throat. To drink, a giraffe must assume an awkward stance and, while lapping up water, it is vulnerable to an attack by a lion lurking at the water hole. But giraffes can go for weeks without sucking up water, depending on the morning dew and the moisture in their food. But when water holes shrink during droughts, giraffes become more vulnerable than other animals, for giraffes cannot dig for water in riverbeds or find moisture in low-growing, drought-resistant plants.

Giraffes rest during the heat of the day, sometimes sleeping while standing up, although they may occasionally lie down for naps, with head and neck draped across the flanks, eyes only half-closed and ears twitching. A giraffe spends about 16 to 20 hours a day browsing, consuming up to 140 pounds of food each day. It adds salt to its diet by sucking up saline dirt, much as it sucks up water, with a neck-down, spread-legs posture. But when eating earth, it raises its head to chew.

Giraffes live in small herds that are widely scattered, keeping in sight of each other even though they may be a mile apart. Herd members are easily identified at a distance because each one has a recognizable reticulated, or net-like, body pattern, and even human observers can learn to tell them apart.

Although conspicuous on the open plain, the giraffe's mosaic pattern camouflages it in trees, the spots merging with the shadows of the forests and its legs resembling tree trunks. So varied is the skin color and the patterning of blotches, ranging from reddish to chestnut brown, that giraffes were once considered to have radiated out into several species or sub-species. Now scientists recognize only one species, with giraffes' body patterns differing from area to area

Able to see across a wide vista from on high, the giraffe has the best vision of any big African animal. Long black lashes shade its large eyes against the sun. It can also close its nostrils against the dust of the arid plains. Because their feet allow them to walk only on firm earth, they cannot cross swampy ground. Rivers are thus natural boundaries for herds.

Lions rarely attack adult giraffes, which can kick viciously when defending themselves or their young. But calves frequently fall victim to the roaming predators.

Although giraffe bulls are not territorial, the males in a herd do form a dominance hierarchy when they reach maturity at about four and a half years of age. The top giraffe is the bull that can drive off challengers. In duels, the two combatants neck-wrestle, slam their hindquarters into each other, or swing their heads like sledgehammers, landing blows that can be heard half a mile away. Although a duel may end in an occasional knockout, serious injury is rare. Their skulls are thick-boned.

The dominant bull is believed to sire most of a herd's young, but usually he does not begin to mate until he is eight or more years old. Females are usually about five years old when they first mate. After a gestation of about 450 days comes the birth of one calf (or, rarely, twins) weighing 104 to 147 pounds. The mother gives birth while standing, so the calf drops about six feet to the ground. Tottering on spindly legs, the six-foot-tall calf can stand about five minutes after birth and begins nursing in 20 minutes. Calves are usually a year or so old before they are weaned. They stay close to their mothers for a few months afterward, then enter the adolescent ranks of the herd. As they mature, they assume the lifestyle of the giraffe, in which an animal is both an individual living on its own and a member of a widespread herd.

The okapi (*Okapia johnstoni*), which looks like a horse with a long neck and partially striped legs, is the only other animal on the giraffe family tree. Okapis and giraffes share features: long tongues (long enough for the okapi to use it for cleaning its eyes) and hair-covered head horns. The okapi, an elusive creature of Zaire's dense, damp forest, was not discovered by scientists until 1900.

Pages 90-91
A giraffe skyline graces the vast Serengeti Plain. The herd, in search of high browse, can scatter across a great distance yet keep each other in sight.

*Bull giraffes duel with necks as weapons, twisting (left)
and knocking (right) in tests of each other's strength.
The duels continue until one walks off, usually with
nothing more injured than his dignity.*

*Dining on high, a giraffe feeds on an acacia tree.
Grasping a branch between lower teeth and a
hard upper gum, the giraffe scrapes off leaves.
Or it can use its prehensile tongue and
upper lip to curl around the leaves
and then pluck them.*

*A giraffe baby (opposite) begins nursing as soon as it
can stand on its shaky legs. Young giraffes, about six
feet tall at birth, can run about 10 hours after
birth. Although it keeps its juvenile look for
months (above), it grows quickly, adding
four feet in height during its first year.*

PAGES 95-96
*Adult and young giraffes lope along the Serengeti
Plain, each animal showing a different phase of the
giraffe's stride. For short distances, a giraffe can run as
fast as 35 miles per hour. Young giraffes can outrun
their parents because the young are lighter.*

ZEBRAS

ZEBRAS live and multiply through the power of advertising. When a newly mature filly first comes into a breeding state, sometime between one and two years of age, she struts around the stallions, her tail and neck stretched, ears turned back, lips pulled in, her mouth opening and closing in a chewing motion that is presumably seductive to males. Stallions also advertise—a term that scientists use to describe male and female display behavior. Head high, ears erect, tail arched, a prancing top stallion advertises to other males his dominance and his rights to the female.

A dozen or more males crowd around the filly and fight the head stallion for the right to mate with her. The fights are mostly mimed, but sometimes the duelists will bite each other. Bachelors that decide not to challenge the harem stallion display their submission by squealing, folding back their ears, and making open-mouthed chewing motions.

The harem usually consists of a stallion, several adult mares, and their offspring. The mares—usually about six, although there may be a dozen or more—are formed in a strict rank hierarchy. The size of a harem depends upon the size of the harem's home range. Generally there are only two or three adult males in a stallion group, which is far less stable than a harem.

Challengers engage the harem stallion for five days or so every month for as long as a year, until the filly finally mates with the stallion and conceives. When she enters his harem, other mares show hostility toward her and harass her when her protector is not around. She lives on a kind of probation for a while as she slips into the strict hierarchy. The first mare to join the harem reigns supreme, followed in rank by the second and the third, continuing down to the harem master's latest conquest. The offspring of the mares share their mothers' ranking.

A challenger of a harem master may abruptly end the duel by lowering his head as if he simply happens to be there because he is grazing. The scientific term for this disingenuous conduct (analogous to human "Who, me?" behavior) is displacement grazing.

Colts leave their family harem when they are two or three years old and join a bachelor herd, which may also include older males that for various reasons are no longer in the mating game. A male remains in that herd until he is mature—at about five years of age—and ready to start a harem of his own. Harems, while remaining small assemblies directed by stallions, loosely form into herds that will share grasslands and migrate together.

Zebras have a large repertoire of rituals, including some for greetings. Adult males may approach each other with heads outstretched and ears cocked. Or one may stand erect and wait for the other to approach. Then begins another ritual of touching and sniffing. One or both may indicate aggression by squealing or making a kicking motion. At parting, one or both may kick out at empty space with their front feet. Harem masters have special threat and hazing displays for the controlling of harem movements. In a biting threat posture, for example, the stallion rears back his ears, bares his teeth, and rapidly swishes his tail. But he does not actually bite.

Despite the skirmishing of competitive males and females, the harem is a stable organization, lasting until its master grows old or falls sick. Because a harem may last for 15 or 20 years, bachelor males are usually too impatient to wait for a change or continually challenge a dominant male. Instead, a typically ardent male will snatch a filly in heat from the harem of her birth and start a harem of his own.

After a gestation of 380 to 390 days, the mare goes into labor. Members of the herd hover nearby, and her stallion stands watch. Newborn foals weigh about 70 pounds, can stand within 15 minutes, and suckle in an hour.

The mother and foal live in solitude for a few days while the foal imprints on her. She then allows other herd members to touch the newborn. Through mutual social grooming, siblings begin to establish a deep, lifelong relationship with their new relative. The grooming,

Standing on wobbly legs, a newborn zebra gets nuzzled by its mother (opposite). When a mare is in labor, she lies on her side while the other females remain nearby and the stallion keeps watch. A foal weighs about 70 pounds, can stand within 15 minutes, and is suckling in an hour.

which is also performed by mothers and their foals, involves mutual nibbling of each other's neck, shoulders, and back. Sometimes zebras also show affection by resting together, their heads arranged so that they can see in all directions—and brush flies off each other's face.

The harem master extends the idea of zebras' mutual care by vigorously protecting his mares and their foals, defending them against lions and hyenas. If a member of a herd wanders off for some reason, the harem master goes looking and calling for the missing member. On the move, the entire herd will slow down so that sick or crippled members can keep up.

Home ranges can be as small as 11 square miles in the best habitat to more than 232 square miles for migratory populations. At their home range, zebras engage in a variety of activities, all of which seem to have to do with establishing their ownership. Often choosing wildebeest stamping grounds for the ceremony, zebras queue up to roll in the dust as if they were bathing. They rub against trees, rocks, and termite mounds. So ritualistic is their behavior that centuries of rubbing have worn the rocks smooth and grooved paths around them.

The zebra is sometimes called the African version of the horse, although it is wild and far from domesticated. Zebras, asses, and horses all belong to the same family, but only the zebra bears those unique stripes; these work as camouflage by confusing a predator attempting to single out an individual in a herd. Striping, usually black on white, varies geographically, with zebras living closer to the Equator being more boldly striped.

A longtime member of the herbivore guild, the zebra has adapted over a long time to many kinds of grassland. Zebras are herbivore pioneers and first to enter tall grasslands or wet pastures. Moving in files controlled by stallions, zebras at daybreak cautiously make their way into long-grass pastures, sometimes traveling ten miles before they settle down for the night. Zebras' teeth and grazing tech-

niques make them more efficient grazers than those that follow. They clear off the tops of the kind of coarse grasses that other herbivores find hard to digest. After the zebras have trampled the land and cropped the grass shorter, the wildebeests and gazelles arrive.

Counting animals on the short-grass plains of the Serengeti between December and May one year, scientists recorded what is believed to be a typical wet-season population: 180,000 zebras, 350,000 wildebeests, and 500,000 gazelles. When the grass dries up, the animals and their newborns leave the plains, scattering into smaller groups and searching in the bush country for new grass and water.

Zebras are choice targets for predators, particularly lions, which stake out ambushes at water holes and in the tall grass that surrounds trampled pastures. Zebras graze both during the day and at night, when they stay in one place, alert to the night hunters. Whenever zebras decide to rest, at least one member of the herd will remain awake on guard duty.

The zebra most often seen by tourists and most frequently reported on by scientists is the plains or Burchell's zebra (*Equus quagga*), a stocky, broad-striped animal that stands 43 to 57 inches high at the shoulder and is 85 to 96 inches long from head to tail; it may weigh nearly 850 pounds. Some of these zebras have reversed the standard pattern, showing a negative version—black with white stripes. On the conventionally striped zebras of this species, southern Ethiopia to central Angola and eastern South Africa, the stripes on legs, belly, and hindquarters tend to disappear.

Grevy's zebra, (*E. grevyi*), which roams southern and eastern Ethiopia and northern Kenya, is 98 to 118 inches long with a shoulder height of 55 to 63 inches. Weighing 700 to 1,000 pounds, it is the largest wild member of the Equidae family. Close-set stripes produce a protective optical illusion, blending with rising heat waves and making them appear to shimmer. Hunted and driven off by farmers, it is rarely seen in its former habitats in Ethiopia or Kenya.

In death, the eye of a zebra (opposite) reflects the images of hunters who shot it under a quota system for game animals in Botswana.

PAGES 102-103
A wave of migrating zebras flows across Savute in Botswana. When the year-end rains water Savute, zebras arrive precisely in time to graze the new sweet grass that greens the marshes. Some zebra populations remain in the same home range all year.

Zebra stallions, fighting for the right to mate, duel with feet and teeth (opposite).
Usually such encounters are sparring matches between the stallion running a harem
and a challenger. But the battle may escalate to bites and slashing with hoofs.

Zebras mate on the Serengeti Plain (above). Harem masters have exclusive mating
rights with two to six mares. They usually will remain in the same harem
for life. A bachelor can start a harem by abducting
a female from the harem of her birth.

PAGES 106-107
Zebras drink at a water hole Kenya. Stripes produce a protective optical illusion,
blurring where an individual begins and ends—and confusing predators trying to
pick out a victim. Each zebra has its own stripe pattern.

PAGES 108-109
As a full moon steals the dark in Botswana, zebras face the dangers of lions that
prowl the night. Some heads are always up so that eyes are
watching when a herd grazes.

WILDEBEESTS

WHILE THE populations of many large African mammals have declined in the last several decades, the number of wildebeests has dramatically surged. An estimated 1.5 million migratory wildebeests inhabit the Serengeti Plain. This is the greatest concentration of wild grazing mammals on earth. Wildebeests form the principal prey for the lions of the Serengeti, but wildebeests are far more than food for lions. They are fascinating animals.

There are two species of wildebeest, also known as gnus: the black or white-tailed wildebeest (*Connochaetes gnu*), which lives in central and eastern South Africa, and the blue wildebeest, also known as the brindled or white-bearded wildebeest (*C. taurinus*), whose range runs from southern Kenya and southern Angola to northern South Africa. Just as they vary in coloration and range, the two species come in several sizes, ranging from 260 pounds to 600 pounds. Most studies focus on the blue wildebeest, whose coloration actually is grayish silver. Most blue wildebeest males grow no larger than 500 pounds, and to a height at the shoulder of about 52 inches. The wildebeest, which belongs to the antelope family, looks like an assemblage of animals. Its long, thin legs are like an antelope's. Its head and large horns give it the look of a bison. Its tail is as long as a horse's. And it sometimes grunts like a frog. Of all the strange new animals that Dutch settlers confronted in South Africa, this was the wildest and strangest. They called it *wildebeest*, the "wild beast."

For a long time, wildebeests' behavior was not understood. The antics of the male earned them the title of clown. Theodore Roosevelt, writing about one of his African safaris, accurately described a blue wildebeest, but neither he nor anyone else at the time understood what they were observing. "As one approaches a herd of wildebeest," Roosevelt wrote, "they stand and gaze, sometimes snorting or grunting, their heads held high and their manes giving them a leonine look. The bulls may pace up and down, pawing the ground and lashing their tails. Then, as the hunter comes nearer, down go their heads and off they start, rollicking, plunging, and bucking.... or a bull will almost stand on its head to toss up the dust with its horns...."

What Roosevelt saw, according to modern animal behaviorists, was a male's reaction to a stranger who had entered a wildebeest stomping ground, a well guarded territory in a complex society. The male who performed for Roosevelt was a bull that was territorial. His initiation into the wildebeest society began when, at about the age of one year, he left the herd of his birth to become a member of a bachelor group. Two or three years later he went off on his own to stake out a territory. As a solitary male, he stayed in the same spot, challenging invaders and waiting for females to wander into his territory.

Solitary males stand like sentinels scattered around the grassy plain. They defend their land through ritualized displays, thrusts of their horns, and calls that sound like "gnu." They are defending a territory whose bounds are not discernible to people. To human eyes, the vast plain seems endlessly the same. But to the owner and to the invader, the territory is specific, its boundaries as well defined as those marked off by a human being's picket fence.

To maintain his position of dominance, a territorial male must continually prove himself in the challenge rituals, which are highly stylized skirmishes, each consisting of as many as 30 motions and lasting from one to 15 minutes. Although males are equipped with formidable horns, they rarely use them to inflict wounds. Nearly always the ritual is bloodless. It is also relentless, for challengers appear almost daily.

The challenger begins his campaign with a bold act of trespass. The territory holder may then "cavort," shaking his head violently and going into a frenzy of spinning, bucking, kicking, and leaping. The invader may then slope off. But if the challenger engages the territory holder in a ritualistic duel, that stylized fighting may go on day after day. If the resident male tries to ignore the newcomer, he becomes confident. He advertises his boldness, marching around to show off to other wildebeests. Then

Migrating wildebeests churn the dust during their annual search for grass and water. They travel more than 800 miles from parched fields to green ones.

he starts to taunt the resident by going through the motions of establishing his own stamping ground. He paws, defecates, rolls around, and digs his horns into the dirt. If this new ritual is not disputed by the resident, the newcomer is on his way to driving off the territory holder.

A male that gives up his territory also gives up his chance to mate. He becomes an outcast in a bachelor herd made up of adolescent bulls and males that have relinquished territory because they could not get or hold land. They gave up because they were psychologically or physically weak, and, in the stern logic of wildebeest behavior, such males cannot father the next generation. The outcast males of the bachelor herd are banished to the outer fringes of the herd, where they become targets for lions and other predators.

When the adolescents in a bachelor herd mature, they will leave and begin their own quest for territory. Males and females reach sexual maturity at a year, but it usually takes three and a half years for a male to become powerful enough to stake out and hold a territory. Females are not territorial. Groups of females, sometimes a thousand strong, wander around the males' territories. As a male approaches the females, he grunts and walks with a stiff, rocking canter, lifting his chin and lowering his ears if he wants to mate. He also shoos away many of the females, along with any calves that stroll into his territory.

The territorial behavior of wildebeest males is vital to the species' continued existence. By shooing away some of the females and their calves, the males keep the herd broken into small groups, spreading out the grazing over a wider area. By forcing bachelors and non-territorial males to the edge of the pasture land, the territorial males lessen the competition of the females and calves for choice grazing areas. The bachelors are also sentinels. If one of them spots a predator, he snorts and raises his head in a special alarm posture. And if a lion kills him, his death is no loss to the herd's gene pool. (Lions have more success catching wildebeests than any other large prey.)

The mating of wildebeests appears to be timed so that the eight-to-nine-month gestation period ends when the rains arrive in a given area—November to January in South Africa, January or February in the Serengeti. Most births occur within two or three weeks before the beginning of the rainy season. Mating and gestation are so precisely synchronized with future rains that one researcher suggested the lunar cycle may somehow be involved in the onset of the mating urge.

The concentration of births during one short period helps preserve the young, for they arrive when the herd is arrayed to protect them and when rain assures the wildebeests of verdant grazing lands. Calves that are born out of birthing season, particularly during migration, are immediately easy targets for predators.

Wildebeest calves can stand within minutes after birth and can run soon afterward. If a mother feels threatened, she can interrupt birth until the danger passes. She can also hold back the afterbirth—an attractant to predators—until the calf is able to run. She then discharges the afterbirth and runs off with her calf. Calves only a few days old can keep up with a running herd. Wildebeests, which have been clocked at speeds up to 50 miles per hour, can frequently outrun predators.

Wildebeests share grazing land with other species in a complex arrangement designed to preserve both the grazers and the land. Wildebeests that remove plant litter in one grazing season may hasten the growth of new plants the following spring. Zebras break down some plants, exposing leafy food for wildebeests. Their grazing, in turn, helps to produce the short grasses the gazelles like to eat.

People slay wildebeests for their tough hides, which make strong leather, and for their tails, which are used as fly whisks. Zulu medicine women also wield the tails as divining tools. Hunters nearly wiped out the black wildebeest in South Africa during the nineteenth century, but preservation and reintroduction efforts by the government and private conservationists, have saved the species.

A wildebeest survivor emerges from a river during migration (opposite). In the panicky crush as they crossed the river, wildebeests had drowned by the dozens

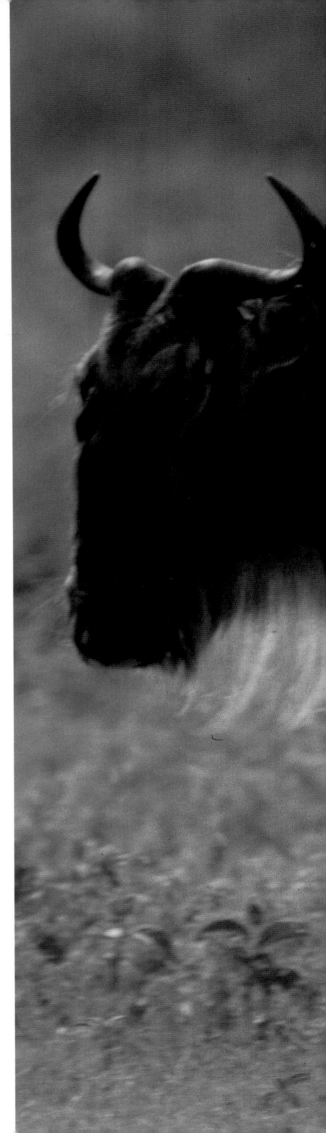

Birth (top) is a vulnerable time for wildebeest newborns and their mothers. Minutes after birth, an infant is on its feet, and soon it is nursing (above) and able to run. Within a few days it keeps up with its mother (opposite) as she rejoins the life of the herd.

PAGES 116-117
Wildebeests thunder down a hillside during their annual migration from the drying May grasslands of the southeast to the flood plains of Lake Victoria and Kenya's bush country. A million or more wildebeests, gazelles, and zebras make the trek, returning eight months later in another massive surge.

A crocodile (above) snatches a wildebeest crossing a Serengeti river during an annual migration that for crocodiles is an annual feast. Thousands of migrants fill the river (opposite) at a spot where crocodiles wait. Wildebeest calves, which have never seen crocodiles before, often are the first into the water—sometimes with a shove from wiser elders.

PAGES 120-121

A wildebeest herd grazes in the temporary peace of a Serengeti sunset. When night comes, cows and calves will gather in tight groups while territorial bulls, holding their ground, become solitary targets for carnivores prowling the darkness.

ANTELOPE

Antelope belong to the order Artiodactyla (hoofed, even-toed animals) and the family Bovidae, which includes buffalo, cattle, goats, and sheep. They are all put in the same family because they share biological and behavioral characteristics. All, for example, are ruminants: They chew the cud, meaning that the food they swallow returns from a stomach chamber for a second chewing. They eat grass by twisting stems around the tongue and cutting off vegetation with their teeth.

Long, short, curved, straight, twisted, spiraled, spiky—the magnificent horns of Africa's antelope serve to identify them to each other and to humans trying to sort them out. But why all these horns in all these different shapes? Scientists believe that it all began with short, spiky horns that evolved through frequent mutations. Animals have always used their horns for dueling, and the victors' horns were part of the genetic heritage of each species.

Horns, which vary considerably among individuals in species, have other purposes. The bongo uproots plants with its horns; the oryx has been known to wield its rapierlike horns against lions; the gemsbok uses its sharp-tipped horns for defense. Most males species swing and thrust their horns in duels for dominance.

Beautiful horns long have attracted hunters, whose quest for trophies wiped out one species, the blue buck, around 1800. Hunting pressures still continue to endanger several species. Yet Africa still has more antelope species and more antelope than any other place on earth.

Antelope range in size from the eland, the largest African antelope—bulls weigh as much as 2,000 pounds—to the little dik-dik and the suni, or pygmy antelope, which is about 12 inches tall. All are prey. Eagles and jackals kill dik-diks and sunis. Lions and hyenas hunt down elands and impalas.

Some antelope roam such isolated areas that their existence was not known to science until recently. Mountain nyalas were discovered in their highland habitat of Ethiopia only in 1908. Antelope that live in dry areas need certain plants that will provide them with water. The long-necked gerenuk (*Lithocranius walleri*)—also known as the giraffe gazelle—seems to need no water. Gerenuk have been seen browsing near water and rarely going for a drink. A gerenuk, sometimes standing upright on its hind legs to browse, seeks plants whose leaves retain moisture.

The sitatunga (*Tragelaphus spekei*), practically lives in water, for its habitats are marshes and lake backwaters. The big, shaggy-haired antelope walks around squishy ground on long, banana-shaped hooves, feeding on reeds.

The typical antelope society has three classes: solitary males, bachelor herds, and nursery herds of females and their young. Most antelope live in grassland or scrubland on which they establish territories, which an adult male defends. Territorial males often "advertise" their status to females by standing on a hill or termite mound, posing for hours.

Antelope territorial behavior has a direct effect on reproduction, for it controls sexual competition. Because property holders must stand in place, females must go to them. This prevents melees in which reproduction would depend more upon chance encounters than on a strict system that awards reproduction rights to strong and persistent partners.

A look at the society of the impala (*Aepyceros melampus*) gives a general view of how territorial antelope live. A dominant male holds a territory that may encompass about half a square mile. He marks it by urinating and defecating along its boundaries. By holding territory he controls a harem consisting of dozens of females and their young. The impala bachelor herd's members include older males that have given up the territorial life, young bucks waiting for the time when they can challenge a dominant male, and yearlings expelled from their birth harem. They were expelled because, by beginning to show interest in females, they threatened to disturb the harem.

During the dry season, impala harems and bachelor herds unite in large herds that search for green vegetation. In the wet season (which

Graceful curving horns crown a male greater kudo (opposite). The horns can grow to 70 inches.

Sassabies, also known as tseesebes (opposite), graze on dew-dappled grass that is turning golden as the rainy season nears its end. They, along with many other species, time their conceptions so that most births come with the rains.

in parts of eastern Africa means much of the year), the sexes separate. Females and their young, forming herds that may number as many as 100 individuals, graze in a home range that covers a couple of square miles. The female herds sometimes join together in a clan that may have 30 to 150 members. Neighboring clans do not squabble or make boundary claims, but there is little interaction among clans.

The males, meanwhile, make their own arrangements. About a third of them will manage to get a territory, either by claiming a piece of the land and defending it against challengers or by challenging and deposing a territory holder. Rarely do encounters end in injury or in death. Males that lose a territory return to a bachelor herd, which has a home range like that of the females.

A territorial male tries to take control of female herds that enter his territory. He expels the young bucks, which are usually about six to nine months old, and sends them off to a bachelor herd. He then busies himself at two tasks: finding a mate and fending off rivals.

Rapidly flashing his tongue and uttering hoarse, loud grunts, he approaches the females, which crowd around him. Most males in the area run off, but one or more may stand his ground. This is a clear challenge to a duel.

Lowering heads and aiming their lyrelike horns at each other, they hurl themselves into battle. Fighting forehead to forehead, they lock horns, each risking a broken horn. Twisting and shoving, they struggle in a ritual that is supposed to produce triumph and humiliation but not injuries. Usually, the struggle ends with both males exhausted and one of them submitting to the other. If the territorial bull triumphs, he remains in charge of his land and his harem. A vanquished challenger either tries again or, giving up, enters a bachelor herd.

Impalas live in open country from Kenya and southern Angola to northern South Africa. Mating and births occur through most of the year among populations whose range is

in equatorial regions. Gestation is from six to seven months; twins are rare.

Dik-diks, at the other end of the antelope size spectrum, have a vastly different territorial style. Studies in the Serengeti of a common dik-dik species (*Madoqua kirki*) showed that males and females mate for life. Each pair and its young mark off a small territory that the male defends. When dik-diks are about seven months old, their parents expel them. After little more than a year, females, and presumably males, are sexually mature. Little more is known about this elusive animal of the dry bush country.

Much also is still to be learned about the sexual behavior of antelope. Why, for example, do some territorial males make a peculiar lip-curling expression when females mill around him? The expression, known as flehmen, opens specialized olfactory receptors near his nasal passages. He can thus detect hormones in a female's urine, which may be a chemical test for mating. Males themselves seem to be chemically inspired, for bulls appear to use a flehmen test to assess each other's hormone level. Territorial males may produce more testosterone than males that are not land holders.

Thomson's gazelles, often called Tommies, mark territory by rubbing grass stems and low bushes with a secretion from glands near their eyes. If a grazing Tommy senses that a predator is near, it sometimes reacts with a springing gait called stotting, from an old Scottish word meaning to go by leaps. Stotting rapidly spreads through the herd as a prelude to galloping flight. Tommies have been clocked at nearly 50 miles per hour.

The gemsbok (*Oryx gazella*), one of the oryx species, has a special talent for finding faraway rain. Creature of desert and arid plain, a gemsbok trekked nearly 56 miles in 18 hours trailing after rain. Scientists who observed gemsbok behavior believe that the animal tracks rain by walking in the direction of fresh plant growth. Gemsbok once were killed for their sharp-tipped horns, which hunters used for spear points. Modern hunters of trophy animals nearly wiped out some populations.

PAGES 126-127
In a touching portrait, an impala mother and her infant share a bonding moment. Young nurse for five to seven months. Females and young form their own herds, which enter areas controlled by territorial males. They eject young males and select females for a harem. Only male land holders can mate.

PAGES 128-129
Impalas line up for a drink at a precious water hole in Botswana, where water can be scarce. Unlike some other antelope species, impalas must drink every day. Wiped out in much of their southern range, impalas have been introduced in some areas.

The nose of an eland (above) is a landing strip for an oxpecker. An eland, although built like an ox, can leap over five-foot obstacles and run at speeds better than 40 miles per hour.

Dik-diks (top), named for their alarm call, stop to listen for danger. They are so small that an eagle can take them. Bonded for life, male and female establish a territory for themselves and their young.

Leaping for their lives (opposite), impalas vault from an area where they sense danger. An impala, startled in open woodland or savanna, can leap as far as 20 feet, springing high in the air even when there is no obstacle in the way.

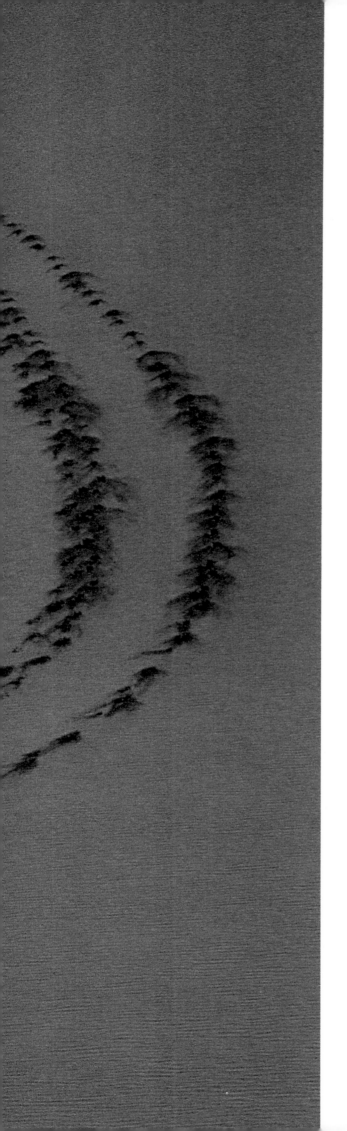

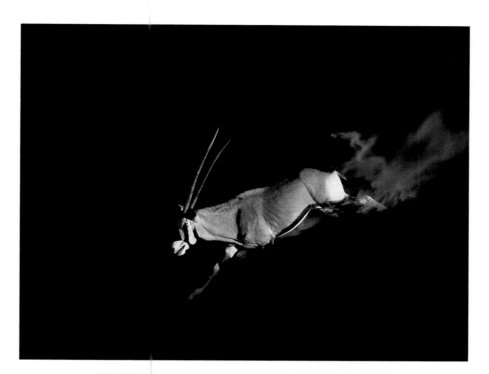

A newborn topi, standing near its mother (above) in a Serengeti grassland, arrived during the rainy season, the best time for food and water. The new topi will quickly begin to keep up with the herd .

Rapierlike horns identify the gemsbok, or oryx, (top), speeding down a dune in the Namib Desert of Namibia. Gemsbok can go for weeks without water, getting necessary moisture from vegetation.

Three gemsbok (opposite) pivot in unison in the Namib Desert. Their tracks trace the pattern of the abrupt, sharp turns that prey use to evade predators. By turning tightly, the prey gets inside the broader turn of the predator and veers off in another direction.

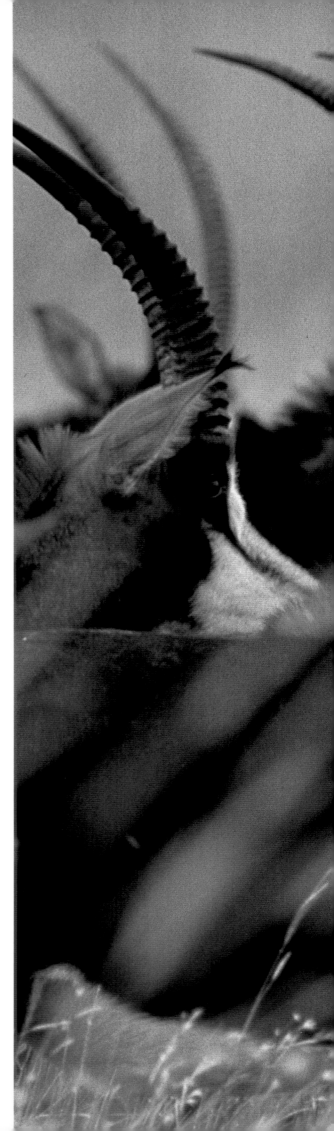

Standing on its hind legs, a gerenuk—also called the
"giraffe gazelle"—stretches to seven feet (above) to
browse on Serengeti brush. Instead of water to
quench its thirst, it relies on moisture in plants
and kidneys adapted to scant liquids.

Sable antelope, whose magnificent horns make them
trophy hunters' targets (opposite), are protected from
extinction but not bullets in Botswana's Moremi
Game Reserve. Rock paintings show that Stone
Age hunters sought the sable antelope's ancestors.

THE GIANTS

T HE BIGGER they are, the harder they fall. That old adage tragically applies to Africa's imperiled wildlife, for three of the continent's giants—the elephant, the rhinoceros, and the Cape buffalo—are all imperiled. They also are all being helped, for conservationists in Africa and elsewhere in the world are vigorously working to preserve them. Extinction has been stalking giants through most of the twentieth century. By the 1970s, the march to oblivion seemed inevitable. Places where elephants, rhinos, and buffalo once roamed by the tens of thousands became killing zones for poachers.

Elephants, in particular, were being wiped out by ivory hunters. Early in the 1990s a worldwide campaign began to stop the trade in tusks. With more than 100 nations united against the ivory trade, the slaughter of elephants began to end.

Trophy hunting still went on, but in Zimbabwe ranch owners discovered that they could make more money aiding hunting safaris than they could by raising cattle. When the fences came down and livestock no longer competed with wild animals, grazing habitats opened. Hunters still killed elephants, but the unfenced land was a boon to the surviving giants.

Africa also discovered the treasures of tourism—people were more than willing to pay to see the giants. South Africa turned over nearly six percent of its land to parks and wildlife reserves. In one of them live about 400 of the 2,400 black rhinos still believed to exist. In a large swath of Botswana wilderness, large herds of Cape buffalo thrive, along with 60,000 elephants. Conservationists, knowing what has happened in modern Africa, look upon that wild land in Botswana and call it the last of Old Africa.

PAGES 136-137
Bull elephants tramp the Ngorongoro Crater, the 10-mile-wide caldera of an extinct volcano in Tanzania. They fear no other animal—except the human species, whose war on the elephant almost wiped it out. Stopping the ivory trade helped to prevent the extinction.

A titan that seems to step out of a scene from the prehistoric Earth, the black rhinoceros competes for space with humans in a land where once he had no rivals.

ELEPHANTS

THE AFRICAN elephant, the largest animal to walk the earth, is also one of the widest-ranging mammals, making a living in tropical forest, on broad savanna, in semidesert, and on the slopes of East African volcanoes. *Njogu*, as the Kikuyu of Kenya call the elephant, has shown an extraordinary ability to adapt to habitat and to climate. In modern times, however, the diminishing Njogu has been forced into a new habitat: parks and refuges created by people who are protecting the elephant from extinction. Fears of extinction were greatly eased in 1990, when an international ban on ivory cut down on the killing of elephants for their tusks.

Two kinds of African elephants roam in pockets south of the Sahara: the bush elephant (*Loxodonta africana africana*) and the smaller forest elephant (*Loxodonta africana cyclotis*). Most studies have focused on the bush elephant—Njogu, the magnificent creature that symbolizes wild Africa.

Awe for the elephant translated into statistics: 10 to 13 feet tall at the shoulder, weighs seven to eight tons, able to eat 500 pounds of food a day, has a life span of 75 or 80 years. The incisor teeth on each side of the upper jaw grow to form tusks, the record being 11 feet long and weighing 236 pounds.

Far more remarkable than the statistics are the facts that researchers have discovered about how elephants behave as individuals and as a members of a society. Many stories have been told about the elephant's extraordinary ability to sense what it could not see. Research by biologists Katharine Payne and William Langbauer now shows that elephants can communicate across distances of several miles through infrasound. Elephants also make at least 15 audible sounds as they growl, roar, trumpet, squeal, and snort to pass information to each other. They have been seen and heard using this repertoire to warn of predators, find stray calves, or keep track of each other.

Elephants are gregarious, sometimes gathering in groups of more than 1,000. They are also prolific. A population in a good habitat can increase by four to five percent annually. Some populations migrate, seeking green land in the dry season, but if food and water are available, most will stay in one place year-round.

Most elephants are members of a herd led by a large, dominant female. Sometimes two or more herds, with all members kin, will unite into a female-led clan, which may grow to as many as 70 members. Outsiders are not welcome. When a newcomer tries to join a clan, the matriarchal leader, with ears flared to add to the illusion of her size, steps forward. With a loud trumpet, she drives off the would-be interloper. Herds are organized around sets of females and their calves, sometimes together with their elder daughters. The matriarch rules until her death. She is usually succeeded by her eldest daughter.

Although births can take place at any time, in most populations nearly all calves are born during the rainy season, when they will be assured of food and cover. Ovulation may be stimulated by a change in diet from the drought season's low-protein dry grass to the rainy season's high-protein grass. After a gestation period of about 22 months, a calf weighing 198 to 265 pounds is born. The herd waits and guards the mothers while they give birth. The pause lasts for two or so days while the newborns gain strength to walk with the herd. Mothers generally nurse only their own calves, but all females will join to protect the young.

The herd often can be heard before it is seen, for the mothers keep trumpeting for their calves and the calves keep bleating in response. Elephant mothers have been seen disciplining their young by slapping them with their trunks or even pulling up a small tree and using it on them like a switch.

Males may not reach sexual maturity until they are teenagers or even 20 years old. Whatever their age, when they are mature, the females expel them from the herd. The males establish bachelor groups or join one already formed. Bachelors continually compete for dominance. They may stage a duel, going through a series of ritualistic gestures—swinging

After a trek of 300 miles, an elephant revels in the water of the Chobe River in Botswana. Elephants can drink as much as 30 gallons a day

Tamping down the ground (opposite) and smashing through the land in search of prodigious amounts of food, elephants may move 30 to 40 miles from one day to the next, leaving devastation in their wake. In clearings made by elephants, plants flourish, a new habitat forms, and lesser animals get a place in the sun.

out their ears, raising the head and trunk, making false charges, and perhaps poking at each other with their tusks. Some old bulls choose a solitary life or are forced into one when they lose their dominant status.

Males become more aggressive when they compete over a female. The fierce—and sometimes fatal—fighting seems to be triggered by a sudden surge in the males' testosterone levels. In extreme form, the condition is known as musth, a sexual state that makes a male unpredictable and uncontrollable. A male begins experiencing an annual musth binge when he is about 25 years old. An outward sign of this violent mood is a watery discharge running down his face from glands near his eyes.

During the days or weeks of musth—a period that seems to coincide with the end of the rainy season—the male stomps and trumpets and subdues any challenging male. He also is drawn to a female herd. He may be summoned, via an infrasound love call uttered by a particular female that is in a breeding state and has known him for a long time. His erratic, aggressive behavior makes him strangely attractive to her. And he is accepted by the matriarch, the guardian of the herd and the judge of what adult male enters it. After the mating of the musth-seized male and the female of his choice, he continues to guard her from other males.

Males 35 years or older may stay in musth for as long as five months. Thus, the passing on of genes from one generation to the next depends upon musth-inspired breeding and results in the mating of old, experienced males with young, selective females.

During the years of elephant killing for ivory, poachers targeted old males with big tusks—the very males most destined to deliver genes to the herd. The ivory hunters also influenced the genetic future in another way. In search of males with perfect tusks, the killers eliminated timid males from the gene pool. Their tusks were unblemished because they never wielded them in duels.

Most human beings feel an inexplicable empathy toward elephants, investing them with human virtues and human feelings. "We can scarcely believe what we see," wrote ecologist Harvey Croze after witnessing a herd's reaction when one of their members lay dying in Tanzania's Serengeti National Park. The old female slumped to the ground. A male lay his tusks against her, struggled to lift her, but could not. He pulled up a patch of grass and placed it by her mouth. Then he tried to mount her, as if trying to breed. After a while, she heaved over and died. For hours, members of her herd visited her body. Finally, a female remained, as if on watch. She trumpeted and, far off, the herd answered. She touched the body one last time and then trudged off to rejoin the herd.

To find food and water, some elephants migrate several hundred miles, from permanent water sources at the start of the rainy season to another permanent water source when the rains end and water holes dry up. The routes of many of these long migrations, handed down as a clan's heritage, have been lost as more and more elephants are killed or put behind the fences of parks and reserves.

Elephants behind fences must learn hard lessons. Normally, elephants throw their weight around in their search for food. They prune savanna brush on a gigantic scale, tear down trees, and crash through thick woods to reach water holes. This creates habitats for smaller animals. They get new paths to trod, newly trampled land on which to graze. In forests, elephant tree-tearing opens the land to the sky, creating glades for a host of animals. Even in death an elephant changes the environment, for as the great body decomposes, toxic fluids kill the roots of certain trees, producing another clearing.

In a human-run reserve, however, elephants must be controlled and even killed to maintain a balance between the needs of the herd and the needs of the habitat. Many young elephants have been plucked from the wild to a park. They act like human teenagers without parents. One park, trying to control them, has added old bulls in the hope that they will show the youngsters how to behave.

*PAGES 144-145
Mother and calf stand for their portrait in Botswana, homeland of some 60,000 elephants— the largest collection of free-living elephants in the world.*

*The massive head of a bull elephant emerges (above)
from the Chobe River in Botswana. In the dry season
tens of thousands of elephants gather along a 60-mile
stretch of the river and swim across to seek the grass in
Namibia. Less protected there, they feed at night
and return to Botswana at dawn.*

*Dust billows around an elephant in Namibia
(opposite). Dirt that showers down on the elephant's
hide acts as a kind of sun block and a coolant.
Elephants can maneuver their trunks in endless
ways, thanks to their many trunk muscles.*

PAGES 148-149
*On the move in the Linyanti Swamp of Botswana,
elephants stay in family groups, with mothers and
young following matriarchs and a few lone
bulls joining the assembly.*

PAGES 150-151
*Big and small meet at a water hole in Botswana.
Impalas line the edge, lapping the shallows. An old
bull elephant lumbers in the mud, his trunk
searching for the water that he needs
more than do the impalas.*

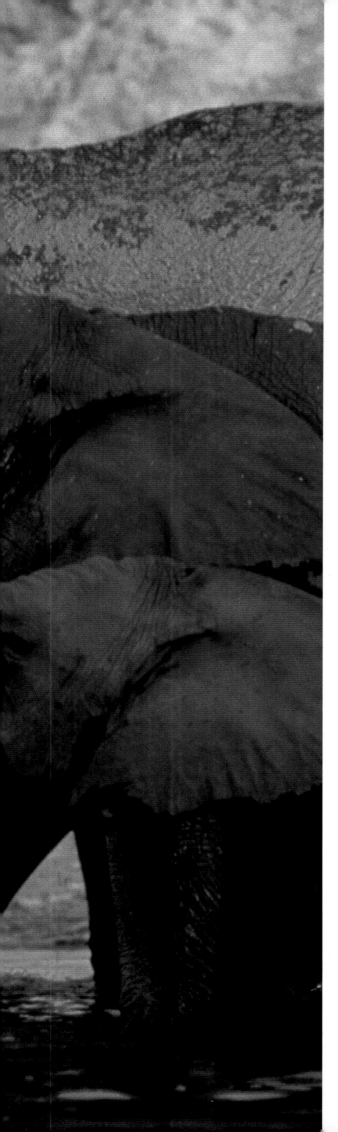

*A newborn elephant (above) toddles along with his family group.
Others will slow their pace so that the youngster can keep up.
At maturity, young bulls leave the group to live
on their own or join other males.*

*At a water hole in the Okavango Delta in Botswana, an infant
(top) slurps up water with its mouth because it has not yet
mastered control of its wobbly trunk. Several months of practice
are needed before a baby begins to make the trunk bend to its will.*

*A youngster tentatively tries to maneuver its trunk (opposite) as
its family group pauses for a drink at the Chobe River in
Botswana. Eventually the youngster will be able to use its
trunk for water and dust baths, for feeding and,
some day, for spanking misbehaving offspring.*

PAGES 154-155
*Under a hunter's moon, bulls gather at a water hole in Botswana.
Peace is more prevalent than aggression in the elephant society,
which is based upon family groups of cows and their young.*

RHINOS

THE BLACK rhinoceros (*Diceros bicornis*) is an enormous animal, 12 feet long, nearly six feet tall at the shoulder, and weighing as much as one and a half tons. Rhinoceros gets its name—"nose horn" in Latin—from its huge double horn, a massive structure anchored in bone and soaring in a pyramidal mass nearly two feet tall. A second, smaller horn juts behind it. Sometimes a third horn grows behind the second.

The horn is a dangerous weapon. Female rhinoceroses wield their horns to defend their young. Rhinos, easily disturbed by a sound or smell, have charged people, stabbed them, and tossed them into the air. Witnesses tell of rhinos charging campfires and overturning trucks and cars. The huge beasts seem instinctively to react to an unknown smell or sight by charging at it. Rhinos lumber around at about two miles per hour but can reach speeds up to 30 miles per hour when they charge.

Rhinos, living in the borderland between savanna and forest, spend much of the day shouldering their way through thorny brush. They waddle along tunnel-like paths between the water, where they drink and bathe, and the green places, where they browse. Egrets often accompany them and tick-eating oxpeckers bedeck their backs. At their water spots or mud wallows, they sink their bodies as deep as they can, seeking relief from heat and flies and ridding themselves of parasites that cling to their bodies. Wallowing in mud, they coat themselves with it. When the mud dries, it forms a protective shield against sun and insects.

Rhinos feed mostly on twigs, bushes, and vines, with occasional fruits. Acacia trees are among their favorite browsing stops. A rhino gathers twigs with its prehensile upper lip and then snaps off a mouthful with its teeth. Rhinos usually sleep during the middle of the day, feeding on morning and evening prowls. Other stops include mineral licks and water holes to wash down meals.

About one third of all of Africa's surviving black rhinos live in protected areas of Tanzania. Others are found, sometimes as subspecies, in small pockets through parts of their former range, which spanned eastern and southern Africa and in the north as far as northeastern Sudan and Nigeria. A few dozen are believed to exist in Cameroon and Chad. Others live in the shelter of a 10,000-acre refuge, the Ngare Sergoi Rhino Sanctuary, which is part of a cattle ranch in Kenya. Cattle share the ranch with the rhinos, lions, antelope, and giraffes. An electric fence surrounds the sanctuary, which is patrolled by armed guards. Ngare Sergoi is a haven for rhinos rescued from poachers, who kill the rhinos for their nose horns. (Powders made from nose-horn shavings have long been used as an aphrodisiac or for medical use in China and India.)

There were 65,000 black rhino in Africa in 1970; today there are only about 2,400. The decline began when European colonists appeared in Africa in the nineteenth century and began to hunt the rhino for sport and for its hide and horn. One black rhino subspecies in South Africa became extinct when the last one was shot in 1853. By about 1900 there were no black rhinos in western Africa. By the 1960s they had disappeared in most of Ethiopia and Somalia.

Rhinos often have been maligned as stupid—a rhino's "short suit is brains," Theodore Roosevelt wrote. But recent research has shown that black rhinos communicate both through various squeaking sounds and differing patterns in their heavy breathing. Males and females have been observed in courting rituals accompanied by a kind of whistling call.

Rhinoceros social arrangements are only dimly known. A good habitat can support a relatively large population. As many as 25 rhinos may reside in an area encompassing little more than a square mile. Within a habitat, a male will show others that he is the occupant of a certain area by urinating along its boundaries. Groups using the same wallow or water hole know each other and stay in the same area, joined in what one observer called a clan. They apparently identify each other by picking up individuals' scents as they tramp through

A white rhino has a gentler disposition than the black rhino. But charm does not count. This rhino species, with 7,000 in the wild, is less endangered than the black.

communal dung heaps. These odoriferous landmarks are surrounded by a shallow furrow that one of the rhinos makes with his horn.

Females stay together. A mother with a calf may also be accompanied by an older daughter. Females without young usually find the company of other females. Young rhinos of both sexes have their own groups. Mature males either go off on their own or make up a temporary group whose members feed and wallow together.

The mother-calf pairs are particularly vulnerable to predators until the calf is old enough to fight off an attack. Hyenas will stalk and harass a mother and her calf, continually trying to move in to snatch the calf. If the mother can successfully match the persistence of the hyenas and fend them off for a few weeks, the calf can grow until it is too big to attack, and the hyenas will depart.

Sometimes males fight so ferociously over females that one of the fighters kills the other. Once a male and female get together, they spend about four months in a kind of courtship. They eat, rest, and sleep side by side before mating. The female gives birth to an 80-to-90-pound calf after a gestation of 420 to 570 days. The calf remains with her until the next birth, usually about three years later.

The white or square-lipped rhinoceros (*Ceratotherium simum*) is larger than the black rhino but does not have a reputation for ferocity toward people. A male may be nearly 14 feet long, stand almost five feet at the shoulder, and weigh close to four tons. This species is not white. Both rhino species, in fact, are about the same shade of gray. "White" is a mistake. Dutch settlers in South Africa, seeing its wide, square mouth, called the rhino *wyd*, or "wide." In English, the word was corrupted to "white."

That wide, square-lipped mouth suits this rhino well, for, unlike the browsing black rhino, the white rhino is strictly a grazer. Its choice food is short grass, which it crops with its lips. White rhinos of South Africa live in woodlands with stretches of grasslands; in East Africa they live in open forests and plains,

sometimes during dry spells moving a few miles away to swamps along the Nile.

The white rhino seems to have a more complex society than the black. A solitary bull is territorial, marking off his land and waddling around it, interrupting trips to water to challenge other males. He will spray urine, as if to show that he has that right and they do not. The challenges are routine affairs, full of posturing and feints.

Calves are born 16 months after mating. A calf weighs 88 to 140 pounds at birth and may nurse for more than a year. A female usually gives birth every two or three years. Just before a new calf is born, the older calf is driven off. Young rhinos form their own small groups. They will join the sexually divided adult herds when they reach maturity—around age seven for females and 10 to 12 for males.

Females and their calves travel together through home ranges of three to four square miles in good habitats; home ranges are larger in less attractive places. Territorial males may spend much of their lives in prime habitats of less than a square mile. They will not bother females that enter the territory unless one of them is in heat. A male will then try to keep her from leaving his territory and will fight for her. When a territorial male and one of his challengers compete for a female, they fight in earnest, butting heads, charging, and often inflicting injury with their horns.

White rhinos once were widespread in Africa. But they suffered much the same fate as black rhinos, dying in great numbers at the hands of settlers clearing land and hunters seeking the precious rhino horns. They were considered extinct in 1893, but in 1894 South Africans discovered a small group in Zulu tribal lands. Isolated populations slowly built up, and a conservation effort began. By 1980 there were 2,000. By the 1990s people working to help the rhino were estimating that some 7,000 white rhino still existed, but no one would dare predict that the white rhino had been saved from extinction.

With the curious stare of an infant, a young black rhino manages to look winsome. It will stay close to its mother until about its third year.

PAGES 160-161
A black rhino, adorned by parasite-seeking oxpeckers, sounds off in the Ngorongoro Crater, one of the few areas in Africa where rhinoceroses live free and safe. Rhinos communicate with many snorts, bellows, and screams.

A mother and her hefty infant (above) enjoy a favorite rhino pastime—wallowing in the mud—in the protective domain of the Ngorongoro Crater. The fiercely protective mother will charge at a predator head-down, aiming to impale it on her horns.

Two against the world (opposite), a mother and her young are the very core of rhinoceros society. She is a devoted mother, comforting her infant with soft, mewing sounds. When the mother has her next calf, usually about three years later, the older one leaves, to face the world on its own.

CAPE BUFFALO

BIG-GAME hunters call the Cape buffalo Africa's most dangerous animal, a big, tough beast that has earned a reputation for killing those who dare to hunt it. People have survived encounters with lions, but no one is known to have lived through an attack by a charging buffalo.

William Judd, a big-game hunter at the turn of the century, said of the Cape buffalo, "I consider them far and away the most dangerous game. The difficulty of stopping a direct charge... the way they can force themselves through bush absolutely impenetrable to man... make them an adversary worthy of the greatest respect."

Human beings are quickly dispatched by a buffalo, which can easily slash or trample them to death. Buffalo seem to hate people. Old buffalo have been known to stalk and kill people who had not threatened them.

Buffalo are particularly ferocious when attacked by lions. A buffalo can kick a lion to death or fatally gore it with massive horns. Attacked by several lions, the buffalo will struggle for hours, fighting back with slashing horns and powerful kicks. And sometimes the buffalo survives, losing only its tail.

Buffalo are notoriously difficult to kill. Its massive horns shield its brain from the front and sides. Because of its girth and tank-like body, its heart is hard to find—particularly by a hunter being charged. Even a shot through the lung will not stop a buffalo. Wounded, a buffalo is even more dangerous, for it will stalk the hunter even as the hunter tries to find it and kill it with another shot. Hunters have been killed before they could fire that coup de grace.

The principal weapon of the Cape buffalo is a formidable set of horns. The horns of males are linked by a structure that covers the front of his head like a shield. There is no more terrifying sight in Africa than that of a buffalo—head down, nostrils flaring—crashing through thorny brush at 35 miles per hour.

Buffalo fear no animal and have often demonstrated their ability to overpower lions and human beings. But they avoid conflict with the mountain gorilla. Buffalo and gorillas share some heavily forested slopes and saddles in the Virunga Mountains. Gorillas eat the lower stems, leaves, and roots of favored plants; buffalo browse on tall nettles. The two species get along most of the time, and buffalo often use gorilla-made trails to make their way to and from feeding areas. If, however, the buffalo get too close on a trail, gorillas will turn suddenly and fake a charge toward the buffalo, driving them off.

The Cape, or African, buffalo (*Syncerus caffer*) stands 30 to 40 inches at the shoulder and weighs 600 to 1,800 pounds. The wide range in dimensions stems from the fact that subspecies vary in size. Buffalo that roam the eastern savannas grow as much as two times the size of their kin in equatorial forests. And males are also much bigger than females. (A relative, the water buffalo, has been domesticated throughout the world, from China to Italy. But the few attempts to domesticate the Cape buffalo have been unsuccessful.)

Most buffalo herds number about 500. At times, these small local herds will join together temporarily into super-herds of 3,000. Assembled in such large aggregations, they do not establish the same kind of social organization that operates in the herd. Each herd has a dominant male. He maintains his role through ritualistic threats, although sometimes he must attack competing males. All the top male has to do is toss his head to get lesser males to back off. But, confronted by a determined challenger, he will charge head-on, smashing into his opponent. Some of the duels end in serious injury to one or both males.

The complex buffalo society is divided into several classes. Female groups, consist of mothers and their young. Adult males accompany the females during the rainy season, the prime time for mating. Females develop a hierarchy, as do the males. Most mature males belong to bachelor bands. A band has about a dozen members, each one a potential challenger of the dominant male.

Crowned by an egret, a Cape buffalo glowers at an intruder. By noisily flapping away at the sign of danger, the bird gives its host an early-warning system.

Young males and females, not yet sexually mature, separate themselves from adults in juvenile groups. Elderly males join together in a kind of old-age club and keep to themselves. These old males set up a dominance hierarchy similar to those established in all other social units of the herd.

Buffalo depend far more on their hearing than on their vision. Their hearing is so acute that blind animals seem able to live normal lives in their herds.

Cape buffalo gather for a mass movement on an East African plain. Although buffalo usually form herds of 50 to 500, sometimes as many as 3,000 will gather in temporary aggregations.

When the herd moves from one place in the home range to another, leadership may keep changing, with either ranking males or females taking over the front ranks of the herd and guiding it on its journey. Herds do not migrate, but they are continually on the move, coursing in a great circle terrain that supplies their needs—grass to eat, water to drink and cavort in, mud to wallow in, mineral licks, and dense cover. They often trek for most of the day, resting during the hot midday, then stopping to graze from late afternoon into the night.

A buffalo herd usually occupies a large home range, and movements through it involve long, steady journeys of 30 to 60 miles. They plod along at a steady speed of about 3 miles per hour, chewing the cud. Like domestic cows, buffaloes have a chambered stomach for the forming of cuds, which are later regurgitated for further chewing.

In the deep forests of western and central Africa, buffalo do not get together in large herds. Rather, close relatives form groups, with no more than about 20 kin. Little is recorded about the buffalo of the deep forest. Presumably, when the juveniles mature sexually they leave their natal groups and search for mates.

In most places, buffalo mate at all times of the year. But mating often seems to be linked to the rainy seasons. In the Serengeti, for example, rainfall usually is heavy from February to July; most conceptions occur around the end of July. Since the gestation period is about 340 days, births take place around the middle of the next rainy season.

A newborn calf typically weighs about 88 pounds. Males will leave their mothers when they are about two years old. Females stay with their mothers until the daughters become sexually mature, sometime between the ages of three and five. A daughter may remain even after she makes her mother a grandmother. This long mother-daughter bond is the basis for the all-female bands found in buffalo herds.

Buffalo have been hunted ever since ancestors of the buffalo roamed the continent. Those huge-horned beasts, known to paleontologists as Pelorovis, were tracked down by Stone Age hunters who probably trapped them by driving them into gullies, where, bogged down in the muck, they would be killed. In historic times, Kikuyu tribesmen in Kenya used a variation to bring down buffalo, a source of meat and hides. They dug deep game pits near water holes or swamp where buffalo were known to gather. Once trapped in the pit, they were speared.

White settlers greatly increased the toll on the buffalo, much as Americans in the West slaughtered the bison (which belongs to different genus and is not a close relative of the Cape buffalo). Later in the twentieth century, when the sport of big-game hunting drew the first wave of trophy hunters, the Cape buffalo became a favorite target. Stories about its fatal attacks on hunters only served to increase its attraction as a game animal, and its great horns, which can span 60 or more inches, became a cherished trophy.

Even more disastrous than hunting—to the buffalo and other wildlife—was the impact of agricultural development, beginning after World War I. Since then, buffalo and other grazers have competed with livestock, and the wild grazers are losing. Hunting and development have wiped out the buffalo in most of South Africa. Ironically, the buffalo got its name from its large numbers around South Africa's Cape Town and Cape of Good Hope. It lives today in scattered ranges. In western Africa, traditional buffalo home ranges are being crowded out by settlement. Only on the protected Serengeti Plain, where tens of thousands live, can the buffalo be seen ranging freely.

*In a life-and-death drama on the Serengeti (opposite),
two lionesses single out a buffalo and attack it from
two sides. . . . Lions manage to grab a buffalo (top);
another (above) fights off an attack.*

PAGES 170-171
*Charged by a phalanx of buffalo, the Serengeti lionesses
run off, denied their kill. Buffalo usually come to the
defense of their own, lowering their heads to
gouge with their massive horns.*

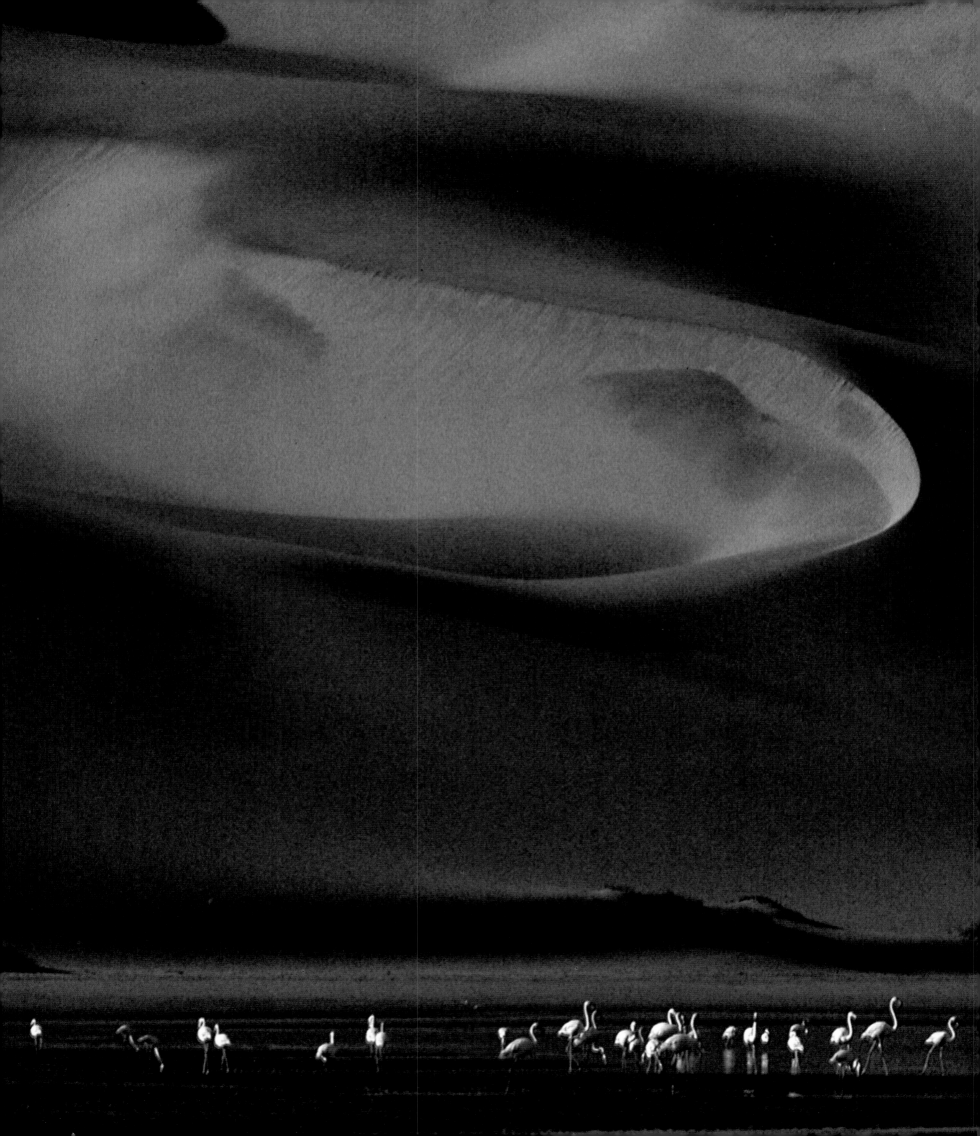

THE BIRDS

"IN THE FIRST misty light of a cool dawn, I was up and straining for a glimpse of the lake.... As visibility gradually increased, I could see a solid mass of pink birds along the shore in front of me. They were lesser flamingos, and so numerous that I couldn't begin to count them." Another day in Kenya begins for ornithologist M. Philip Kahl.

Elsewhere in Kenya, the feathery halo of the crowned crane shimmers in the sun. Food-hunting avocets sweep their upcurved bills along the shore of a shallow lagoon. A red-white-and-blue kingfisher digs a nest hole in a lake bank. A carmine bee-eater swoops down on a brush fire to feed on fleeing insects. On an island off Namibia, jackass penguins make loud braying calls, showing how they got the name. An Egyptian vulture, once thought extinct, courses the skies over Chobe National Park in Botswana.

Kenya is a bird watcher's paradise. An energetic birder can find 100 species in a single day within 25 miles of Nairobi. About 2000 species of birds live in southern Africa (compared to about 650 in the United States and Canada). Another 150 species spend part of the year in Africa as migrants. On Birding Day in November in South Africa, bird watchers can spot 250 or more species within 24 hours.

The late Roger Tory Peterson, the most famous American bird watcher, wrote of sitting on a veranda in East Africa and during one lunch hour seeing what he called a pageantry of birds: red-billed hornbills, golden-breasted starlings, buffalo weavers, fan-tailed ravens. "There is no part of the world," he wrote, "where the bird enthusiast or the bird photographer can enjoy a happier or more successful holiday than in East Africa."

BIRDS OF AFRICA

CREATURES in tropical Africa have had eons to evolve in a relatively steady climate with a dependable wet-dry cycle. Adaptation has produced a diversity of species, especially bird species. There are giants like the ostrich and the pelican, along with innumerable kinds of smaller birds that have found niches from desert to savanna, from mountainside to rain forest. Besides the locals, there are visitors. Hundreds of species migrate annually to Africa from Europe.

Africa's flightless ostrich (*Struthio camelus*) is the largest living bird, standing nearly eight feet high and weighing as much as 300 pounds. A primitive creature built for running instead of flying, the ostrich is a tough old bird. Primarily a bird of wooded savannas, it can also survive in the desert wastes of Namibia's barren Skeleton Coast—so called because of the ship-wrecks that dot the shore. Ostriches usually travel in groups, depending upon keen eyesight and fast running to evade predators.

Males may have a harem of as many as five hens, one of them dominant. They lay two or three dozen eggs in a communal hollow for an incubation of about 40 days. The male takes over the task of brooding the eggs, with some relief from the dominant hen. Chicks can run as soon as they hatch, and run they must, for jackals and hyenas frequently raid ostrich nests. An ancient tale claims that an ostrich tries to make itself invisible by burying its head in the sand. That libel probably was started by a Roman who saw a distant ostrich in its hollow nest, its neck stretched out to lower its profile.

Ever since biblical times people have been fascinated with African birds. The sacred ibis (*Threskiornis aethiopica*) retains its common name from the time when Egyptians worshiped it as symbol of a god. Bird behavior intrigued the historian Herodotus, who claimed that African plovers flew into the gaping mouths of croco-diles to pluck out leeches. This is seriously doubted today, but plovers are often seen run-ning along a croc's back to catch insects. They also bury their chicks in time of danger, squirt-ing water on the sand to keep them cool.

Other avian oddities include the water dikkop (*Burhinus vermiculatus*) which some-times makes its nests near crocodile dens and lays its eggs on the droppings of elephants and buffalo; the open-billed stork (*Anastomus lamel-ligerus*) which has a bill formed like a nutcrack-er to open the shells of snails and mollusks; and the namaqua sandgrouse (*Pterocles namaqua*), which lives in semi-desert areas, flies to far-off water sources, soaks itself, and returns to the nest, where chicks suck water from specialized belly feathers.

African weavers are renowned as architects and builders of complex hanging nests. Of some 140 species of weavers, 89 have been reported in eastern Africa. The weavers' most elaborate creation is produced by the grosbeak weaver (*Amblyospiza albifrons*), which usually suspends its nest between tall reeds. Weaver species use varied techniques and raw materials, but all the birds can tie knots ; and all of them weave exquisitely, producing nests that have the same oval or globular shape. Those that have bottom entrances also have a partition designed to keep eggs from falling out.

Males seem to build compulsively, plaiting nest after nest to lure females. Some species build weaver communities, festooning acacia trees with strings of nests. To ward off preda-tors, the birds often build near the nests of stinging insects or even close to people's houses.

Hundreds of thousands of red-billed queleas (*Quelea quelea*) fill the skies in eastern Africa as the gregarious weavers travel from one food stop to another in raids on farmers' grain fields. Another relative, the whydah or widow-bird, slips eggs into the nests of unsuspecting finches. When the weaver eggs hatch, the chicks mimic the color patterns and even the behavior of the legitimate chicks. The involuntary foster par-ents usually are fooled, continuing to care for the interlopers until they fly away.

Large birds have large appetites, and their demand for food sometimes puts them into competition with other species. The white peli-can (*Pelecanus onocrotalus*), which can grow to be more than five feet long, eats up to four pounds

A grosbeak weaver (opposite) plaits a nest strung among papyrus plants in Botswana. The strong-billed bird makes its own weaving material by grasping the edge of a reed frond and flying off, unraveling a frond strip on the wing.

of fish a day. Groups of pelicans often work together; forming a semi-circle in the water and, rapidly flapping their huge wings, they drive fish toward shore. Then they scoop up the catch with their pouches, their heads dipping simultaneously, as if following the rules for a drill in some avian manual of arms.

When health officials stocked Kenya's Lake Nakuru with fish that ate mosquito larvae, pelicans found a new fish to eat, consuming the newcomers by the ton. At another lake, thousands of pelicans in a search of nesting sites drove off thousands of flamingos. Of all of Africa's spectacular bird species, flamingos gather in the greatest numbers. Two species often share a habitat—the greater flamingo (*Phoenicopterus ruber*) and the lesser (*Phoeniconaias minor*). The lesser, three feet tall, is about half the size of the greater.

When a million flamingos gather at Lake Nakuru, they consume 180 tons of food a day. The two species can eat together without competing, because each chooses a different food. The greater eats mollusks, tiny crustaceans, and tiny aquatic animals, while the lesser dines on algae and diatoms. Both search by moving their heads side to side and sucking up water. As the water is expelled through the closed large, curved bill, the food is filtered through a fringe of tissue that acts like a strainer. Each species has a filter that strains the foods of choice. Flamingos sometimes browse in highly alkaline water that could be fatal if swallowed in quantity. While eating in such waters they regularly go to springs to drink freshwater.

At breeding sites around lakes, flamingos build mud nests one or two feet high, with a dip in the top to support an egg. Chicks hatch in about a month and wander around in the huge forest of legs, looking to the casual observer as if they are on their own. But behaviorists have noted that a parent only feeds its own chick. Parental feeding—the regurgitating of food into the chick's mouth—continues until the young bird can fly and find its own food.

Uganda has made the crowned, or crested, crane (*Balearica regulorum*) the nation's emblem.

This beautiful bird with its feathery crown may also be an emblem of birds in danger. Long ago its existence was threatened by milliners seeking its feathers for ladies' hats. Now the threat comes from the draining of marshes, a widespread land reclamation effort that has drastically decreased the crane's habitat. Attempts have been made to breed the bird in captivity to preserve the species.

Crowned cranes mate for life. The pairs belong to a large flock, which includes young birds. During the breeding season, each couple goes off on its own. Male and female tramp down a space amid reeds and work together to build a nest in which two or three eggs are laid. Both parents care for the young. Cranes often perform a wild, wing-spreading dance, leaping high into the air. The reason for the dance is not known, since they are permanently mated and have no need for courtship.

The African fish eagle (*Haliaetus vocifer*), a small, white-headed raptor, also mates for life. The male and female spend relatively little time aloft. Like human fishermen, most of their time is spent waiting, perched near each other on a tree alongside a lake or river. An eagle can grab a small fish with one claw; heavier prey is seized in two claws.

Storks have a more varied diet. Some hunt locust and grasshoppers in open fields. Others walk around in lake shallows, fishing. Africa's most numerous stork, the marabou (*Leptoptilos crumeniferus*) is notorious as a scavenger in villages. And some, in company with vultures, eat carrion.

Vultures are built to dispose of carrion. The Ruppell's griffon vulture (*Gyps ruppellii*), has a hooked bill for tearing into a carcass. Its neck and head lack feathers, making it easier and less messy for poking into a bloody body. Vultures know how to get what they want. They even use tools. Jane Goodall, watching an Egyptian vulture (*Neophron percnopterus*) on the Serengeti Plain, saw it try to break open an ostrich egg with its beak. The bird went away, returned with a stone, and repeatedly threw it down on the egg until it cracked open.

Sprinting in the Serengeti (opposite), an ostrich shows the powerful legs that propel it at speeds of 30 miles per hour for 15 minutes or more. In short bursts, it can reach nearly 45 miles per hour.

An ostrich (above) guards a communal clutch of eggs
in a nest hollowed out in the sands of Botswana's
Makgadikgadi Pans. Conspicuous in size and
plumage, ostriches depend upon speed to save
themselves from predators.

High stepping ostriches kick up the dust (opposite) in
the birdland of Botswana, where photographer
Frans Lanting once counted 28 avian species
at one pool of water.

*Bearing the feathery crest of its name, the crowned
crane (above) struts and flies throughout Africa.
It appears on the coat of arms of Uganda. In flight,
as here over Senegal (top), the crane utters a plaintive
cry. The gregarious birds sometimes assemble in flocks
of 100 or more. A treetop in Kenya (opposite) gives
three a platform for their stately profiles.*

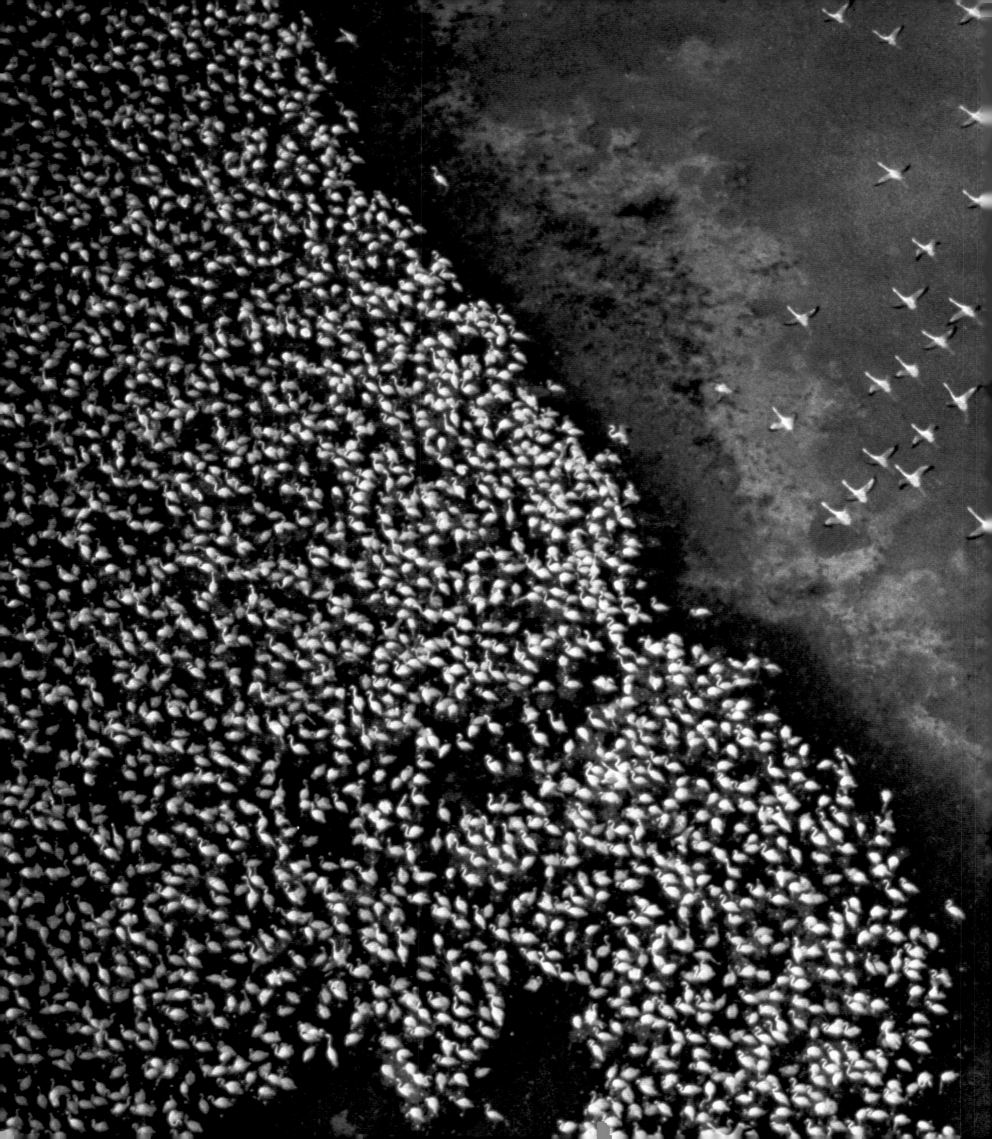

The flamingo's eating maneuver—stand and sweep for watery fare—is aided by a sinuous neck (above) and filtering bill, which lets water out and keeps food in.

Clusters of flamingos form living islands (opposite) as they feed and fly at the Makgadikgadi Pans. The salt flat in Botswana becomes a lake when rare rain fills it, luring hundreds of thousands of flamingos.

White pelicans bathe and drink in Tanzania (above).
Migrants of the wide-ranging species, from Europe and
Asia, often join the African pelicans, but birds that
breed usually remain as permanent residents.
During breeding season the male's plumage
changes to pink; his face turns pinkish
yellow, the female's bright orange.

*A yellow-billed stork, carrying nesting material
(above), returns to its colony in Botswana. Pinkish-
white plumage has a touch of crimson during
breeding season. A fishing bird, it often raises
one broad wing, probably to block the sun's
glare while it looks for fish.*

Vultures in a tree scout for food (above). They hunt for the dead by watching for predators gathered at a kill. Sometimes as many as 100 vultures crowd around a body, snatching carrion fare with hooked beaks suited to tearing into a corpse.

Eye on the prize, an African fish eagle (opposite) flexes its claws, moments from a strike. Sharp claws will dig into the fish, which the eagle then drags along the water until it takes off and flies to a tree for a leisurely meal.

THE WATER DWELLERS

A POOL OF precious African water is a little world, separate from land yet still dependent upon it. Fish live on what they can find. Many leave their world, clutched in the claws of an eagle or impaled on the rapierlike beak of the long-necked snakebird. Turtles of the pool find niches where they lay their eggs. Hippopotamuses, eating elsewhere but coming back to the pool each day, provide fertilizer. Hippo dung supplies nutrients to bacteria, insect larvae, and crustaceans—the lowest links in the long food chain of the pool.

Crocodiles are also major members of the water community, but their presence is not entirely benevolent to others. Here is a familiar scene: the crocodile comes, slips into the water, and begins to hunt, with eyes low in the water and its movement almost imperceptible. Near shore, a hippo mother turns her back on her calf. The croc's hunt is over in moments. It seizes the calf and drags it under to drown. The results of the croc's acts are not all lethal, however. Fishes and turtles get scraps from croc kills. And birds, riding on the crocodile's back, get moving perches from which to hunt for insects.

In coastal waters from Mauritania to Angola, humpback dolphins and dusky dolphins swim and leap. Off the coast of South Africa in spring and summer, bottle-nosed whales give birth to calves. Along the beach of a South African park, sea turtles find sanctuary and a place to hide their eggs from human harm. On the Atlantic coast of Namibia, fur seals swim out of the sea to breed on warm beaches. These, too, are the water animals of Africa, a land whose seas, ponds, lakes, and rivers sustain a rich variety of life.

A bullfrog enjoys water newly come to its habitat in Botswana (opposite). For months the frog had lived in a kind of suspended animation under the sands, waiting for the annual rains.

HIPPOPOTAMUS

L UMBERING along on land, a two-ton hippopotamus looks comically awkward. But when a hippo slips beneath the water and becomes almost weightless, it moves gracefully, its feet barely touching bottom as it swims around, tiny ears folded in, nostril slits closed, eyes open. Water is the hippo's true home.

Hippos spend most of the day in or near water, sometimes submerging for three or four minutes at a time. Like many large animals, hippos do not have an internal way to regulate their body temperature. So they seek external relief by cooling down in water or in mud wallows. From specialized pores oozes an oily pink substance that keeps the hippo from drying out on land or getting overly soaked in the water. This protective secretion is sometimes called "blood sweat," but it is neither.

A hippopotamus (*Hippopotamus amphibius*), a vegetarian that grazes with lips nearly two feet wide, can consume as much as 200 pounds of grass, herbs, and leaves a night, the time when hippos prefer to eat. Returning to its watery home from a night of foraging on shore, a hippopotamus becomes the major life force in the pool. Fish nibble algae from the hippo's hide. Walking about, the hippo stirs up the compost on the bottom, mixing fertilizer and vegetation. Clouds of food rise, feeding the fish that will in turn become the food of birds and turtles. Pools with resident hippos have far more aquatic life than pools lacking the huge mammals.

Hippopotamus populations can be large. Researchers counted 6,544 along a 102-mile stretch of the Luangwa River in Zambia. Another study found an average of seven hippos along every 1,000 yards of a lake shore and 33 occupying every 100 yards of river bank. The hippos in these habitats form groups under a bull. He claims a territory where he gathers a harem of several females and their young. Territories encompass a strip of shore and water.

The dominant bull in an area controls the best habitat. He gets that prime territory by defeating challengers in duels that ratchet up from ritualistic display to bloody battle. A duel usually begins with the dominant bull rearing out of the water, opening his enormous mouth, and letting out a roar. That fearsome sight and sound may be all that is needed to drive off a challenger. But if the rival stands fast, the next encounter becomes a real attack. Both bulls smash into each other, slamming their jaws together. During the duel, which may last an hour or more, they slash and bite, inflicting deep wounds with their sharp tusks. Sometimes the duel is a fight to the death, with only the ruler or challenger left standing. Scars on the bodies of bulls attest to the brutality of the fights.

To keep his females for himself, a bull will fight off any hippo that dares to come near, even a young one that is not a sexual rival. Males are so ferocious that females often form their own nursery herd, or crèche, to guard the calves.

Most hippo breeding takes place so that the gestation period, 227 to 240 days, will end when rainfall is at its peak. A calf weighs 50 to 100 pounds at birth and will weigh about 500 pounds by its first birthday. Calves, which nurse underwater, can swim before they can walk. Mothers let them crawl onto their backs, possibly as a way to keep them from the jaws of crocodiles. The females watch over their young in shallow water and will lash out in warning to protect their young, sometimes acting as aggressively as males. Protective mothers have been blamed for capsizing boats and attacking the passengers, sometimes fatally.

Hippos may sometimes form large herds that include adult females and calves. There seems to be little stability in such groups, which usually break up after a short time. Herds may be formed under the duress of drought, when hippos must seek a home at another river or lake. If the trek there is a long one, many may die.

Females and their young usually have lasting relationships. Adult females have been seen frequently with youngsters of different ages, some of them probably the offspring of other mothers. Solitary males—some of them losers in duels, others young bulls driven away from a father's harem—live at the edges of the habitat, well away from dominant bulls.

Ready to charge a rival, a hippo rears from a watering hole in Botswana's Savute River (opposite). A duel for supremacy may end in a jaw-to-jaw battle with razor-sharp tusks as weapons.

PAGES 195-196
Oxpecker on its back and Egyptian geese at its feet, a hippopotamus dominates the landscape of the Serengeti. Hippos usually spend daylight hours in water or muddy wallows, moving at night to grazing sites.

PAGES 197-198
An angry Serengeti hippo becomes a mud slinger. Aggressive males are territorial, fighting off rivals with roaring, charging displays—or with a bloody, jaw-to-jaw battle. A duel may last for hours until one gives way—or dies.

CROCODILES

ONE LOOK at the toothy African, or Nile, crocodile (*Crocodylus niloticus*) and you know that it lives on meat. When it hunts, a muscle seals its throat shut so that it can open its mouth underwater and seize prey. African crocodiles often hunt prey too large to swallow. Because of their dental and jaw structure, they cannot chew. So they must tear the victim apart, twisting or even spinning in the water to rip off a piece.

In a typical attack, a croc grabs an animal by a leg and pulls it under, where the dismembering begins. The croc's jaws can clamp down with an estimated ton of force, but they can be held closed by a person willing to try.

Sometimes several crocodiles will feed together, each holding onto the prey while twisting their bodies. This allows big pieces to be torn off for easier swallowing. In such mass feedings, territorial bulls, as dominant animals, tend to get more food than subordinate ones.

Food, gulped down in large chunks, is digested with the aid of "stomach stones" that the crocodile picks up from the bottom of a lake or river and then swallows. Muscles contract the stomach, moving the stones around to grind up the food. Sometimes a crocodile stores a dead animal away by wedging the body between underwater rocks or under submerged branches. The crocodile then waits until the flesh decomposes, making the tearing easier. Some scientists describe this storing of carcasses as a primitive form of tool use.

One of the world's largest carnivores, African crocodiles can easily kill big prey, including human beings. Some African villages protect themselves against crocodiles by building stockades around the shores where people wash clothes or fetch water. Crocs measured in the Grumeti River of Tanzania have been 18 feet long; they weighed nearly a ton.

African crocodiles often scavenge from carcasses, at times peacefully joining with other hungry animals. Crocs also have a reputed tolerance for certain bird species. Supposedly, spur-winged plovers enter the gaping jaws of crocodiles to feed on parasites or pick pieces of meat from between the formidable teeth. Reports of such bird behavior go back to ancient times, but many scientists are skeptical.

African crocodiles live in lakes, rivers, freshwater swamps, and can tolerate brackish waters along the coast. With their snouts and feet they dig dens as refuges in times of drought or temperature drops. They communicate among themselves, using hisses and cough-like sounds during mating rituals, to warn of intruders, or to indicate distress. There probably is much more to their repertoire, but their communication system is still little understood.

Females and males become sexually mature when they reach a length of about eight feet. Breeding times vary geographically, with females beginning to dig anticipatory nests during the dry season in the north, and at the beginning of the rainy season in the south, usually from November through to the end of December. The female lays 30 to 50 fertilized eggs in a nest covered with sand or dirt and leaves. Through 70 to 100 days of incubation, she stays near the nest. But she must leave occasionally to cool off in the water, a vital necessity, for crocodiles must continually regulate their temperature. While she is temporarily away, predators raid the nests.

When chicks are ready to hatch, they peep. Drawn to them, the mother scratches away the nest covering and helps them find their way to the water. The little crocs will remain near their mother, perhaps for as long as two years. She may form a crèche with other females so that all the young are in one area. But the young are essentially on their own—potential prey until they grow big enough to ward off predators including, bulls, which will attack and even eat young trespassing crocs.

The young crocodile's first meals are water beetles, crabs, other small aquatic invertebrates, along with spiders and insects. Soon the growing crocodile is taking fish, birds, snails, frogs and other amphibians. By the time the crocodiles are full-grown adults they are killing antelope, buffalo, and young hippos, and perhaps an occasional python draped on a tree near shore.

A crocodile bares its teeth during a sojourn out of the water in Botswana. Although he presents a frightening visage, he may well be opening his mouth simply to shed heat and cool off.

A crocodile emerges from the wetlands of the
Okavango Delta in Botswana (above). The
croc's teeth—some visible when the jaws
are closed—are arranged for
tearing, not chewing.

*Huge jaws open, a crocodile warns and threatens a
rival in Okavango Delta waters (above). Crocs
are often blamed when someone disappears, but
eyewitness accounts of killings are rare.*

*In a scene that dinosaurs would have seen, a crocodile
crawls out of an egg (above). Its ancestors—some
perhaps 50 feet long—preyed upon dinosaurs
with as much lethal skill as today's crocodiles.*

*Crocodiles often form large assemblies, as here in the
Okavango Delta of Botswana. But they are solitary
hunters, usually floating along with only eyes, ear slits,
and nostrils exposed, ready to pounce on unwary prey.*

SEALS

THOUSANDS OF fur seals live in the waters and along the shores of Africa. These aquatic mammals are encased in blubber and in fur—an inner layer that traps bubbles of air and keeps the skin dry and an outer lair of guard hair that protects them when they haul out on rocky shore. Like terrestrial carnivores, they make a living by hunting. But instead of stalking prey in a rain forest or on a grassy plain, fur seals plunge into the water, where they are as shrewd and agile as predators on land.

The key to their success is their ability to conserve oxygen. As a seal is about to dive, its heartbeat slows down. In some species, this will be an oxygen-saving drop from 55 to 120 beats per minute to 4 to 15 beats per minute. During the dive, many of the seal's blood vessels constrict, while a normal blood flow continues in the heart and brain.. This also cuts back on oxygen needs. Carbon dioxide builds up, but seals can tolerate this. At the end of the dive, the seal sticks its head out of the sea, takes a few deep breaths, and its normal heartbeat resumes.

The southern fur seal (*Arctocephalus pusillus*), the best known African sea mammal, typically dives to about 12 feet and stays down two minutes. But some seals seem to be better or more determined divers than others, diving as deep as 55 feet and staying under for 7.5 minutes in their hunt for fish, crustaceans, squid and other cephalopods.

Southern fur seals spend most of their lives near breeding sites along the coasts of South Africa, Namibia, and Angola. The yearly cycle of life of the fur seal begins in October, when bulls arrive to stake out their territory—patches of rocky shore or sandy beach encompassing 10 to 20 square yards.

The dominant bulls establish boundary lines and sometimes confront each other along the edges of their territories. Because they usually respect each other's boundaries, these territorial bulls rarely fight. But they do attack bachelors that come ashore hoping to dislodge land holders. Young males that have not yet challenged the dominant males live beyond the colony, as do old bulls unable to hold a territory.

Next to haul ashore are the females, many of them pregnant. They settle down in groups, the pregnant ones giving birth to pups conceived a year before. So that pups can be delivered at the ideal time, birth has been held up by a delayed-implantation process: The female's fertilized egg stays in a kind of suspended state for four months before attaching to the uterus and beginning actual gestation, which takes about eight months.

Dominant bulls, maintaining harems of as many as 50 females, fast during the breeding season, probably because they dare not risk going to sea to fish and leave their territories undefended. There is always a bachelor ready to try to evict a land holder. Other bachelors may seek places of their own so that they can mate with unclaimed females.

Pregnant females generally go to sea for a short while after giving birth, then return to the breeding site and mate again, beginning a new reproductive cycle.

A pup, which weighs 10 to 15 pounds at birth, will nurse for a year or more. But a few months after birth it will be alongside its mother, hunting for its own food.

After the breeding season, adults and pups return to sea, almost always off the beaches where all of their lives began. They are known to live at least 18 years.

Males become sexually mature when they are only a few months old, but they usually are not able to take and hold a territory until they are about 11 years old. And even then a male cannot expect to hold territory for more than two years. Females reach sexual maturity at four years of age.

Because females only produce one pup a year, southern seals' reproduction rate is low. Yet they have managed to survive the pressure of hunting since 1610. They recovered from near-extinction in the late nineteenth century through regulations designed to make fur seals a perennial crop. Sealers continue to harvest tens of thousands of seals annually, hoping that their crop will always grow back.

Fur seals, clustered on a Namibian beach (opposite), form a breeding colony with a complex social structure. Bulls defend individual territories, while females settle down in groups.

THE PRIMATES

O NE SPECIES of primate—*Homo sapiens*—lives on every continent. Many of the other species—a vast array of monkeys, chimpanzees, gorillas, and baboons—live in Africa, the world's prime location for members of the Primate Order. In one forest on one plateau in northern Gabon, for example, 15 primate species have been found, and two more were discovered in a swamp only 25 miles away.

Out of Africa came our own primate species, and that kinship endures. The DNA of the chimpanzee differs from the human being's only by a little more than one percentage point. The chimpanzee's genetic similarity to human beings has made chimps stand-ins for people in medical and psychological research.

When we look at a primate, we sense kinship, for those mammals that evolved into primates changed their faces. And all primate faces, whether the gorilla's or the human being's, bear a family resemblance. As primate ancestors evolved, eyes moved forward and became more prominent, for the most important sense was shifting from smell to sight. With the eyes in the front of the head, the braincase could expand, allowing the enlargement of the brain. As the brain grew so did its complexity, giving primates intellectual power. Linking this power to dexterous hands, primates became tool users. And, as they sharpened their senses, they became adept at communications and the development of social behavior.

When we see gorillas grooming each other or baboons bonding in friendship, we sense emotions resembling our own. Watching the interplay of power and persuasion in primate societies, we understand what is going on. In primate behavior we see the roots of our own behavior.

PAGES 208-209
Survivor of a diminishing band, a gorilla forages in Volcanoes National Park in Rwanda, where 300 of the world's 600 mountain gorillas live. Conservation work in Rwanda, Zaire, and Uganda has kept the gorillas from disappearing.

Tree-dwelling bonobos, also called pygmy chimpanzees, look homeward in the tropical Wamba forest in Zaire (opposite). Females with their young form the core of a bonobo group. Males and females seem to get along better than their larger cousins.

BABOONS

BABOONS are primates that adapted to life on the ground, walking around on all fours instead of swinging through trees like many other primates. Baboons' arms are slightly longer than their legs, and so their bodies slope backward as they amble along in a rocking-horse gait. Large-headed and muscular, a baboon has a muzzle like a dog, with small eyes set deep under a straight brow. (Its scientific name means "dog"—*cyno*—and "head"—*cephalus*.) A ruff of long, wiry hair radiates around its jaws. Baboons have razor-sharp canine teeth that can be as long as a lion's. A male may weigh more than 100 pounds. Females are smaller than males.

In studies of baboon behavior, scientists have found clues to behavior at the dawn of human evolution, when our ancestors became distinct from the ape line. Genetically, people are much more closely related to chimpanzees than to baboons. But, like our hominid ancestors, baboon ancestors left the trees millions of years ago, and when they adapted to life on the ground they faced problems similar to those that confronted hominids. Seeing the baboons' solution to the relocation problems provides insights into how our own ancestors solved them, imprinting behavioral patterns into the earliest humans.

Baboons know that in unity there is strength. They join together to defend themselves, menacing would-be predators with ferocious displays—teeth bared, head thrust forward, hair raised, eyes rolling, feet stomping. The show of aggression, performed in unison by members of a troop, almost invariably drives away predators. Leopards will not attack a baboon troop, but they will attack one that has wandered off alone. Biologists note that baboons thrive in places lacking leopards.

In the politics of baboon society, males compete among themselves for dominance, as do females. And each troop is also competing with other troops in the baboons' constant search for food and security. Troops, which may include hundreds, consist of baboons that stay together each night at a certain spot, such as a cliff, where they will be safe from predators.

At the core of a troop are family groups of females and their offspring. The females are in a strict hierarchy, with daughters inheriting their mothers' ranks. Each mother heads a matriarchal line in which offspring are ranked according to age, the youngest first. It may take two years or so for the ranking female to achieve and enforce her status, but once she is acknowledged, she has top rank for life.

Some observations have shown that dominant females give birth to young that have better chances of surviving than do the young of lower-ranking females. But often these matriarchs will have more miscarriages than subordinate females. Some scientists believe that there may be a hormonal basis for the connection between dominance and lower fertility, the result being a natural limit on the number of potential matriarchs in a troop.

Studies of the olive baboon (*Papio anubis*) in Kenya showed that female bonding preserves the troop, for females stay in the troop for life while mature males migrate from one troop to another. In olive baboon troops, as in ape and monkey groups, the family unit is always the same: a mother and her young, including immature males. Mothers spend most of their time with their young but also form lasting friendships with troop members that are not kin. Females make friends with other females and with males, both during and outside the breeding season. But males never make friends with males.

The olive baboon, named for its olive-brown coat, lives in savannas from Mali to Ethiopia and northern Tanzania and in mountainous areas of the Sahara. Other species include the western baboon (*P. papio*) of Senegal, Gambia, and Guinea; the chacma baboon (*P. ursinus*) of southern Africa; and the yellow baboon (*P. cynocephalus*), a widespread species found from Somalia and Kenya to Angola. The hamadryas baboon (*Papio hamadryas*), worshipped as a god in ancient Egypt, is believed to be extinct as a wild creature in Egypt. It is rare in its last

In a threatening signal, a male baboon (opposite) bares his canines and shows the white above his eyelids. Other threat signals include staring, slapping the ground, and erecting the ruff around his mouth, making himself look bigger.

A baboon, safe from non-climbing lions, contemplates life from a tree (opposite). Its ancestors—and ours— moved from the trees to a more hazardous life on the ground.

homeland, Ethiopia, where much of the baboon habitat is giving way to agriculture.

All baboon species have similar social structures, with local variations. The typical baboon day begins when the troop leaves its sleeping site and divides into bands that forage for food. Within the band of 30 to 90 animals there are several units consisting of one male and several adult females with their young. As the bands forage, two male-led units may unite, often with the younger male taking the lead, followed by females and young. Thus the most vulnerable position is taken by a young male, which the gene pool can afford to lose, while, at the rear is an older, experienced male whose genes are more valuable to the troop. By protecting females, the males are also protecting the best food gatherers. In many troops, the most aggressive females generally collect the most fruit and seeds.

Troops may also form into a clan of as many as 200 animals, with adult females outnumbering males two or three to one. Mature males leave their birth troop and may go from troop to troop, but they will remain with their clan.

Male-female interplay is continual. If two females happen to begin grooming a male simultaneously, they will scream and fight until one skulks off. Mature females invite mating, signaling their interest by staring with their startling, white-lidded eyes, smacking their lips, and posturing. Young males may respond, but senior males, especially those high in rank, wait to mate when a female is most likely to conceive.

When a female becomes sexually receptive, she begins a temporary relationship with one male or with several in a row. This consortship, as scientists call it, may last for mere moments or for several days. In the consortships of olive baboons (and presumably among other baboon species), males that had formed previous friendships with the female had a better chance of mating than other males. A male's appreciation of baboon courting behavior was far more important than aggression.

Most conceptions take place during the rainy season, when baboons are at their fittest.

The gestation is six months. Newborns ride on their mothers' backs when the troop is on the move. By the time a baby is a month old it can move on its own. Babies learn about group behavior early. Three or four play together in groups formed by mothers with small young. At about a year of age, a baboon can forage on its own, but it stays near its mother until it is at least a year and a half old. Females spend about half of their 20- to 30-year life caring for young. Fathers play no role in bringing up the young.

Baboons will live nearly everywhere—in open woodland, savannas, grassland, and in rocky hill country—as long as they can find water and a safe place, such as trees or cliffs, where they can sleep. And they eat whatever they can find. Troops have been seen methodically canvassing an area, seeking roots, grasshoppers, and fallen fruit. They can become so engrossed with finding food that they become oblivious to predators. They drag honeycombs across the grass to rid them of bees and then eat the abandoned honey. They grab up bunches of grass and beat it on a rock, then gather around to eat the berries, insects, and seeds that have shaken out. They crack one end of an ostrich egg, break it off, and then tip up the egg and gulp down the contents. Some baboons, found along the coast of South Africa, scoop mollusks and crabs out of the shallows.

Baboons, especially males, will also hunt, grabbing and killing hare, birds, dik-diks, Thomson's gazelles, and the young of impala and reedbuck. The hunters share their kills with other males, females, and young. The diversity of their diet is another indication of the adaptability of these primates as is their search for water: Where open water is not easily attainable, they will dig to find it.

The mandrill (*Mandrillus sphinx*), found in Cameroon, Equatorial Guinea, Gabon, and Congo, is closely related to baboons, as is the drill (*M. leucophaeus*), found in Cameroon and the island of Bioko. These largest of monkeys inhabit thick rain forests. When foraging, larger adults stay on the ground, while the young and smaller females browse in the trees.

Holding fast to its mother, a baboon baby in Botswana (above) has entered a new stage of babyhood: a shift from hanging onto the mother's stomach to riding on her back. The baby will nurse for six to eight months.

A hunting baboon (opposite) pulls down a Thomson's gazelle on the Serengeti. Baboons live on fruit, grass, roots, and insects, with an occasional kill of a small animal. One group was seen avoiding all other food for a feast of grasshoppers.

GORILLAS

THE GORILLA, labeled "half-man half beast" in a nineteenth-century account, is big but not vicious. A full-grown male can rear up to a full six feet, thumping his chest with long, powerful arms. He weighs about 400 pounds. Females are smaller and weigh about half as much. Gorillas move around on all fours and seldom walk upright. They can climb trees but are rarely seen swimming, leading observers to believe that rivers and even streams form boundaries for gorilla groups. In swampy areas, however, gorillas will wade into water in search of food.

The gorilla (*Gorilla gorilla*) is a vegetarian with a large appetite, ranging through dense forests in a daily hunt for food. Gorillas may gulp down insects while feeding on plants, but their vegetarianism is conscientious enough for them to avoid such fare as eggs and injured birds.

Some gorillas are solitary, but most are members of groups, which may number as many as two dozen gorillas. The dominant male leads the group, hooting and howling commands to keep the group organized and his subordinates in line. He may reign for years and will probably be succeeded by one of his sons. Males that are not his sons tend to leave as they mature. They will either live alone or join other groups. A loner may wander around until he finds females willing to join him in establishing a new group.

Female gorillas, unlike their chimp and baboon cousins, leave the group of their birth when they reach maturity. A female leaves when she wants to and may join a lone male on her own initiative.

As they lumber through thick vegetation on their daily foraging expeditions, members of groups keep in touch with each other by grunts and barks. Two groups in the same area generally ignore each other. But the group leader of one may decide to advertise his mighty presence to another group by staging an elaborate display. He hoots loudly, stands to his full height, and pounds his enormous chest, which is nearly six feet in circumference. The pounding, with cupped hands, is loud, rhythmic, and ends when the gorilla begins to run around and crash through the forest. Such displays, when seen by humans, probably inspired the gorilla's unwarranted reputation as a raging beast—a reputation that in movie myth produced King Kong.

Gorillas have an elaborate communications system based on a large repertoire of sounds and displays. The hoots, one of about 20 different sounds, are audible half a mile away and seem to be aimed at interlopers. In time of danger, gorillas suddenly become silent. That seems to be an extremely effective signal, for it alerts the group to danger but does not reveal any locations.

A dominant male leading a foraging group will indicate his choice of routes by standing up, facing in the direction he had chosen, and then scanning the group, looking at each one in turn. If he senses that any of them did not heed him, he will tap that gorilla and once more look in the chosen direction.

Several scientists have studied gorilla communications. The gorilla Koko, for example, learned to sign more than 500 words, such as "teeth" as she looked at a photo of a grinning chimpanzee. Other signed words, showing that she was afraid, sad, happy, or angry, indicated self-recognition, a quality deemed to be essential to high-level communication. Whether Koko and other signing gorillas were actually using language is still a matter of debate. Skeptics say that the gorillas are simply demonstrating conditioned behavior.

Most gorillas inhabit lowland rain forests, but a subspecies, the mountain gorilla (*G. g. beringei*), lives in the dense forests of extinct volcanoes—the highest 14,787 feet—that make up the Virunga Mountains straddling the Zaire-Rwanda-Uganda border. Much of what we know about the mountain gorilla came from Dian Fossey, who began studying them in 1967. She wrote *Gorillas in the Mist*, which was eventually made into a film.

The gorillas at first ran screaming at the sight of her, but they gradually drew close, even touching her, after she learned to mimic their gestures and calls. Each group she observed

A young male gorilla takes a midmorning rest in Volcanoes National Park (opposite). When he and the others in his group end their rest, they will forage and travel until nightfall.

Hands of a young mountain gorilla grasp a dead tree in Volcanoes National Park (opposite). He is eating the bark. Young males called blackbacks are led by mature silverback elders.

had a home range of about five square miles. They traveled over part of it each day, usually following trails that led to favored eating places and nesting sites. They ate vines, bamboo, wild celery, ferns, thistles, nettles, tree bark, and berries. Each day ended with members of the group building leafy nests and going to sleep. The nest is not used again.

An older male, called a silverback for the silvery hair across his back, led each group. Dian Fossey kept watch on nine groups, whose membership varied from five to 20 males and females. Each silverback leader had around him subordinate males that served as sentries or guards of the females, juveniles, and infants. Once, she noted, when a juvenile temporarily lost its mother, the silverback took the youngster under his care, allowing it to share his nest.

Dian Fossey determined that the character of a group frequently depended upon the character of its leader. She was on hand to see what happened in a group after its silverback, Whinny, died. Leadership was assumed by the group's number two silverback, Uncle Bert. "He clamped down on the group's activity like a gouty headmaster," she wrote. "The gorillas' previous calm acceptance of my presence was replaced by chest beating, whacking at foliage, hiding, and similar activities showing alarm. Nervous and excitable in his new role, Uncle Bert led Group 4... into more remote areas where interference from both humans and other gorillas was minimal."

Females begin mating at about age 10, males at age 15. A female gives birth about every three and a half to five and a half years; during her reproductive years she will have two to three surviving young. A gorilla infant, smaller at birth than a typical human baby, nurses for nearly two years but begins learning about edible plants at about three months by watching what its mother eats. Everything the baby learns comes from watching its mother or other members of the group. An infant usually sleeps with its mother until it is about three years old or until she gives birth again.

In the middle of the day the group pauses to rest in quickly made day nests of bent foliage or branches. While infants play—sliding down dirt banks and tree trunks is a favorite sport— the adults rest and groom, picking bits of dried skin or foreign matter from their own or another's hair. (They dislike water, but will wade to get food.) Sometimes several infants are watched over by one female while the others go off to feed or sun themselves.

One day, hearing "a soft hoot bark" nearby, Dian Fossey climbed into the crotch of a large tree and tried to make herself inconspicuous; a gorilla she had named Peanuts was approaching, and she hoped to meet him. "Lying back among the leaves, to appear as harmless as possible," she wrote, "I extended my palm. Then slowly I turned my hand over and let it lie.... What seemed an interminable time went by as Peanuts put out his furry hand and gently touched his fingers twice against mine.... For that fleeting instant a bridge, spanning a chasm of immeasurable time, linked our two species."

On another day she found a massacre: five gorillas had been killed—"mauled by dogs, pierced by spears, and battered by stones, apparently just for the excitement of the hunt." The sight infuriated her. So did the land hunger of herders and farmers. As poachers killed gorillas and as others chipped away at the ever-shrinking habitat of Peanuts and the other gorillas she had learned to love, Dian Fossey turned from objective scientist to fierce ally of the mountain gorilla. Transformed from scientist to savior, she made enemies. In December 1985 someone entered her cabin in Karisoke, where she had set up a research center. The assailant, who would never be brought to justice, slashed her to death.

Her scientific observations were unique and valuable. More valuable was the fact that her passionate love of the mountain gorillas focused world attention on a species in great danger. When she went to the mountains in 1967, biologists estimated that only 250 mountain gorillas existed. In 1993, there were 600, including 300 in what is known as Uganda's Impenetrable Forest. That increase in population was her legacy.

PAGES 222-223
A hungry lowland gorilla wades toward sedges that grow in Nouabalé-Ndoki National Park in Congo. Photographer Michael Nichols spent 21 days on a platform to make this photo—evidence that gorillas, long thought to be leery of water, will dunk at least to eat.

*Papoose embraces Pasika, her seven-month-old baby
(above). The two will share a nest each night until
Pasika is about three or until Papoose has another baby.*

*Members of the Titus Group take an early morning rest
on Mount Karisimbi (opposite). Titus plays with
Pasika. Titus deposed Beetsme, an adolescent
when Dian Fossey named him in 1975.*

PAGES 226-227
*Pasika, safe in mother's mighty arms, looks out on a
world with the gentle, inquisitive eyes of a baby. Such
moments capture the appeal that reaches out from
primate gorilla to primate human.*

CHIMPANZEES

IN 1960 a young English woman named Jane Goodall arrived in Africa to begin what would become the longest field study ever made of an animal group in the wild. During her three decades in Tanzania, she and her research team have discovered more about our close relatives than had been known in all of human history. She found that chimps could use tools and that, like us, they had a dark side. Some war on their kin and some kill their young. But, most of them, she says, "care about each other, help each other, show compassion for each other."

A chimpanzee she later named David Greybeard was the first chimpanzee to let her get close. When David Greybeard wandered into her camp and took bananas, his companions were poised for flight. Then, she later reported, "they would look at David, their eyes would get very big, and instead of running off, they'd stop. David helped me open a door into a magic world."

On another day, she sat next to him when he stopped by a stream. "I saw a red palm nut lying there," she remembered, "and I picked it up and held it out to him. He didn't want it. There was something wrong with it perhaps. And he reached out and he took it from my hand, and with one smooth movement he dropped it. But at the same time he very gently held my hand and gave it a soft pressure. And that was a communication which could be understood without any need of words: He didn't want the nut, but he understood my gesture in giving it. It was a reassurance."

Such observations jarred scientific convention, as did her practice of giving individuals names. When she went to Cambridge University to continue her studies in an academic setting, she was told not to waste time on the chimpanzee mind because animals did not have minds. Conventional wisdom persisted even after Jane Goodall observed chimpanzees making tools—stripping leaves from twigs to modify them for use as probes into termite nests. In western Africa, Swiss biologist Christophe Boesch and his wife Hedwige

Boesch-Achermann saw chimps using rocks and branches as hammers to open nuts. They also watched chimps teach nut-opening techniques to their young. These eyewitness reports forced science to redefine animal intelligence, since tool-making had been considered a skill developed exclusively by human beings.

The depth of chimp intelligence still is not known, especially in the wild. Chimps have been seen eating leaves of what natives know to be a medicinal plant. Some researchers believe that the chimps eat the leaves to relieve stomach pains or get rid of internal parasites. Chimps also use leaves as sponges to soak up water for drinking and cleansing. They have used branches as hooks to pull down fruit and as weapons in attacks on other chimps.

The first indication of warfare among chimpanzees came in 1974 at a Goodall study area named Kasakela in Tanzania's Gombe National Park. Males of the Kasakela community were fighting the Kahama community, which consisted of seven males, three adult females, and their young. The surprise attacks were bloody. The attackers, perhaps seeing the others as potential threats, may have been making preemptive strikes. The raiders killed their foes and ate their flesh. In four years the Kasakela chimpanzees wiped out the Kahama group.

"I don't believe that aggression is inevitable just because, quite clearly, it is part of ancient primate heritage," Jane Goodall comments. "And remember that just as deeply rooted in our ancient primate heritage are the roots of compassion and love and altruism."

Washoe, a chimp born in the wild and taught American Sign Language, showed the loving side of primate nature. Psychologists Allen and Beatrice Gardner, who reared her, taught her to link signs to make such expressions as "give me a drink" and "open food drink," a request to open a refrigerator and give her something to drink. After working with her for about four years, they reluctantly left her in the hands of a graduate student and, not wanting to interfere with his work, stayed away. One day, after an 11-year absence, the Gardners appeared in the

A chimpanzee (opposite) hangs out under observation at Jane Goodall's research site in Tanzania's Gombe National Park. There she discovered chimpanzee tool use and saw the chimps' dark side in acts of violence against each other.

In the face of a chimpanzee (opposite) can be seen the look of the thinker—the link between them and us. Frodo, a chimp at Jane Goodall's Gobe study site, is the aggressive son of Fifi, rated by Goodall as the best mother at Gombe. Goodall predicts that Frodo some day will become the dominant male at Gombe.

lab, unannounced. Washoe stared at them for a long while, made the name signs for each of them—and then signed "come hug."

Linguists debate endlessly over issues of chimp communication. Can animals that lack the organs of speech engage in "pre-verbal" communication, as a human child would? Is understanding human words the same as knowing what words are? One chimp, for example, follows a command—"Go get the ball that is outdoors"—ignoring a ball that is indoors. Another chimp, taught about numbers, sees a banana cut in half and points to a sign on which "½" is written; it then points to "2," indicating a desire for two bananas.

In the wild—which can be woodlands, grasslands, and rain forests—the chimpanzee (*Pan troglodytes*) usually travels on all fours, flexing its hands so that it appears to get about on knuckles and feet. Chimps also occasionally walk upright. An adult male usually stands about four feet high and weighs about 100 pounds; females are slightly shorter and lighter. Once thought to be vegetarians, they are now known to augment their diet with meat. Individuals stalk and kill young antelope, baboons, and monkeys or even steal kills from baboons. Working together, several chimps ambush bush pigs and adult baboons.

Chimpanzees live in "communities" of males, females, and young. To remain in charge of the community, dominant males sometimes form coalitions. Males will also sometimes elope with a female, staying with her, away from the community, long enough to guarantee that he will be the father of her offspring. Males and females both develop hierarchies. In the shifting dominance of the community, a young male with a high-ranking mother may display dominance over older males.

Jane Goodall describes the community as a "fusion-fission" society in which both males and females have independence, and each develops his or her own associates. A group is usually held together by the presence of females that are ready to mate.

Females do not become mothers until they

are about 13 or 14; it takes a little longer for males to work their way up the hierarchy. Gestation lasts about 230 days and the interval between births is usually five or six years. The young will remain close to their mothers for a decade or more. Mothers and daughters may stay together for life.

Groups of various combinations may form for hours or for days, with individuals roaming off on their own to join other groups. Pairs of community members often strengthen their bonds by grooming each other.

Although males may attack other males—especially those of other communities—much of their behavior is friendly. Frequently a male that comes upon a likely food source will invite other members of the community to the feast with a "food call," one of about 25 sounds that observers have identified as having specific meaning among chimps.

Hunters and planters have wiped out large populations of chimps. Early in the twentieth century there were millions of chimpanzees across a wide swath of the continent. Today there are about 200,000, and that number drops steadily.

Bonobos, pygmy chimps not identified as a separate species (*Pan paniscus*) until 1933, are not that much smaller than the better known chimpanzees. But bonobos have a somewhat different society, which primatologist Takayoshi Kano calls "female-centric." Kano, who has been studying the bonobos for more than 20 years, reports that females form the core of bonobo groups. Males, he says, "do not dominate or lead; they just follow." A bonobo son usually stays with his mother's group for life. Daughters go off to other bands.

About 15,000 bonobos are believed to exist, but they are threatened by hunters, seeking not only meat but also body parts for use in religious worship. The logging of their forest homelands has also fragmented their ranges, making it more difficult for large groups to forage. Bonobos apparently get their name from a variation on the pronunciation of Bolobo, a town in their lowland forest habitat

In the Taï Forest, Côte D'Ivoire, chimpanzees live a natural life (above) while being observed by Christophe Boesche, who discovered that they used rock hammer tools and were hunters of red colobus monkeys. Chimps there hunt prey and share their kill. The group was later decimated by the Ebola virus.

*At a medical research center in Liberia, old and young
chimps embrace (above). There and at other centers
chimps are used for research on AIDS and other
diseases. Young chimps are exempt from
experiments until they are at
least three years old.*

MADAGASCAR

PAGES 234-235
Wide-eyed creature of the night, an aye-aye peers out from its nest high in a tree. Of all of Madagascar's bizarre beasts, the aye-aye baffled scientific classifiers the most, for it has the chisel-like teeth of a rodent, the skull of a squirrel, and the tail of a fox.

MARCO POLO told of a giant bird that could "pounce on an elephant and carry it up to a great height in the air." Arabs called the bird—which bore Sinbad the Sailor aloft in *The Thousand and One Nights*—a roc. An island off Africa was said to be the lair of the roc. To prove that the bird existed, men brought back huge quills from the island.

The mystery of the roc was solved in 1851when scientists reported the discovery on the island of two enormous eggs and a large bird bone. The mythical roc was a real bird, dubbed the elephant bird (*Aepyornis maximus*), bigger than the biggest ostrich and extinct since the 1600s. The gigantic quill turned out to be a frond from a type of big palm tree that still grows on the island.

The fabled place was Madagascar, about 250 miles off Africa's east coast. It still is a realm of odd animals with odd names—lemurs, aye-ayes, tenrecs, fossas—living in a world apart.

The Texas-size island broke away from the African continent about 160 million years ago. In isolation, life adapted here in a burst of evolution. Some 80 percent of the island's plants and animals live nowhere else. But many appear doomed, for Madagascar is burning itself to death. In 1900, a primeval forest covered more than 90 percent of the island. Scarcely 10 percent remains today, as farmers clear new land by burning down trees and brush. Animals crowd into smaller habitats, and Madagascar sets another biological record: Nowhere else in the world are more animal species in danger.

A leaf-tailed gecko (opposite) takes a defensive stance against primates—in this case, the photographer. One of 63 species of geckos on Madagascar, the leaf-tail gets its name from its camouflage technique. Clinging with sucker feet against a branch, it looks like a leaf.

A FADING EDEN

SCIENTISTS who give animals their Latin names sometimes get fanciful. When they named the strange primates of Madagascar, they chose *Lemur*, which comes from a Latin word for spirits of the dead. Romans believed that the lemur spirits hovered at the back of a household hearth and stared through the flames. Animal lemurs also stare, in a disquieting way. Their big-eyed, relentless gaze seems vaguely malicious, or at least eerie. Monkeylike primates of many sizes and habits, they live only on Madagascar and the nearby Comoro Islands.

Madagascar's lemurs, like other animals and plants on this world apart, are here because of the island's unique story. Some 40 million years ago, the island lay closer to the African continent. Across the shallow strait drifted logs and debris from Africa's tropical forests. Like tiny arks, the drifting stuff carried little animals. They were early mammals, inheritors of the world that dinosaurs once had ruled.

As Madagascar wandered farther from Africa, the island's animals began evolving in ways radically different from those of creatures in Africa. There, for example, the earliest lemurs were succeeded by animals that would evolve into apes and humans. On Madagascar, however, the lemurs survived and evolved on their own, forming a variety of species to fill many niches.

Some lemurs spend most of their lives in trees. Others swing from limb to limb, then drop to the ground and hop about like little kangaroos. The smallest, the mouse lemur, is well described by its scientific name, *Microcebus murinus*—"mouse-sized tiny monkey." A dweller in tree holes, it is about five inches long and has a six-inch tail. The largest of the lemurs, the black and white, silky-furred indri (*Indri indri*), is about two feet tall and, in native legend, lives as an animal that can catch a spear and throw it back. While the indri cannot do that, it can walk upright like an ape and has earned itself the native name *babakoto*, "cousin to man."

Some little lemurs have serrated cutting teeth that can gnaw into the bamboo and reeds that the species live on. One of these specialists, the purring golden bamboo lemur (*Hapalemur aureus*), was not discovered until 1985.

The tiny fork-marked mouse lemur (*Phaner furcifer*) gets its name from the pattern of black streaks running down its head. It has found a way to live in a wilderness studded with sharp-tipped pinnacles known as *tsingy*, the Malagasy word for "spikes." A leaping, climbing tree dweller, it eats insect secretions found on tree trunks and limbs. It also scrapes bark to get at resin, another diet staple.

Treetops are the home range of three lemur species known as monkey lemurs or sifakas, so called for their alarm cry—"shee-fak." As a sifaka leaps from tree to tree, its arm membranes flare as a gliding aid. On the ground, they hop. Sifakas like to stretch out on limbs and spend a while sunbathing. Troops defend their treetop territories, which they mark off with urine and scent from a throat gland. When troops meet, they growl at each other and leap ritualistically, as if to cross territorial borders. But they do not fight. The troops appear to be made up of closely related females accompanied by males that come and go.

Madagascar has no large predators or herds of grazers, for the evolutionary ancestors of animals like lions and antelope never reached the island. Unlike the prey-predator life on the continent, life on Madagascar is more a matter of finding a niche. Some animals make a living on the ground, others high in tropical forests, still others in deserts and on high mountain slopes. Evolution produced amazing diversity. The island has thousands of different kinds of plants, including more than 1,000 species of orchids, 80 percent of them found nowhere else. A mountain top may be the world's only site for 200 particular plant species. And the next mountain top may have 200 different species of its own. Madagascar has about 250 species of reptiles, 90 percent unique to the island. Of the 198 species of nesting birds, 106 are indigenous to Madagascar, as are at least 148 species of frogs.

Where there are trees, there are insects living

With a startled stare, a ring-tailed mongoose (opposite) interrupts a prowl into a rain forest. One of the island's few carnivores, the ring-tail hunts small mammals. A good climber and swimmer, it lives in a burrow that it digs in humid forests.

in them and birds to get them out and eat them. But on Madagascar this "woodpecker niche," as biologists call it, is filled by the aye-aye (*Daubentonia madagascariensis*), a big-eyed little lemur that sleeps in a tree nest 30 to 45 feet above ground. The aye-aye is a victim of both habitat loss and superstition. Human beings not only cut down the tall trees that shelter the aye-aye, they also kill it because they see it as devilish.

Going forth by night, the aye-aye flits among the trees in search of food. It puts an ear against a tree and listens for sounds of grubs in decaying wood. The aye-aye then bites into the wood with its chisel-shaped front teeth and inserts a long third finger into passages made by the grubs, hooks one with a fingertip claw, and pulls out the grub. An aye-aye can also bite open a bird egg, insert that long finger and, wielding it like a one-tine fork, rapidly empty the egg. Using this same technique, the aye-aye gnaws a hole in a coconut and eats it clean.

The predator niche on the island is filled by the fossa (*Cryptoprocta ferox*). If any animal on the island is devilish, it is the fossa. Its eyes stare out from a narrow, mustached face, and when rankled it emits a powerful, nauseating scent. Like many other Madagascar animals, the fossa looks as if it were assembled from the parts of other beasts. It has the face of a fox, the eyes and claws of a cat, and the broad feet of a bear. Its lean body, two to three feet long, is covered in a smooth, reddish brown fur, and its muscular tail is as long as its body. Hunting like a solitary cat but treading like a bear, the fossa preys on lemurs, chasing them high in trees and along the ground.

The fossa is one of eight carnivore species, all found only on Madagascar and all of them biologically confusing, for they have characteristics of ferrets and mongooses found elsewhere in the world. Scientists thought that the long-snouted falanouc (*Eupleres goudotii*) was an insect-eater until they noticed that it mainly ate earthworms and frogs. The burrowing ring-tailed mongoose (*Galidia elegans*) also

caused confusion because it has some of the characteristics of a civet. A swimmer, it sometimes dines on fish. The narrow-striped mongoose (*Mungotictis decemlineata*) opens birds' eggs or snail shells by lying on its side, grasping the food container in all four paws, and throwing it until it breaks.

Shrews and moles are missing on Madagascar. Their niche is occupied by the Tenrecidae family, whose 30-odd, mouse-sized species have taken over the island's underground. Each of three rice-growing regions on Madagascar has its own species of rice tenrecs. They pester farmers by burrowing into rice-field dikes, causing leaks. Long-tailed tenrecs, which resemble shrews, have made a wide array of adaptations. Some carve tunnels, others prowl leaf litter. Some can make very unshrewish leaps, using an inordinately long tail for balance.

Tenrecs that live in places having dry seasons can store fat in their tails and go into a dormant state until the rains come again. A web-footed tenrec, propelled by a strong tail, swims after prey in marshes and lakes. Other tenrecs resemble hedgehogs. For defense, they roll into a ball bristling with white-tipped spines. One species hibernates for as long as five months. A streaked version has a row of spines along its back. By flexing and quivering the crest of spines, adults produce faint sounds used for communication in the darkness of their network of tunnels.

Conservationists have been working for decades to save Madagascar and its unique array of life. The basic strategy is to show the people that by saving the environment they can earn money through eco-tourism. Changing old ways is exasperatingly difficult. Generations of families have survived by hunting and by destructive land use: charcoal burning and simply moving on when soil is exhausted, then clearing new land by burning trees and brush. So widespread is the burning that astronauts orbiting in space can see the smoke and the rivers clogged with mud, washed down newly barren hills.

A crowned lemur pauses during a scamper across the pinnacles of a Madagascar landscape known as tsingy, *the Malagasy word for "spikes."*

PAGES 242-243
Shooting from the lip, a Parson's chameleon snags a grasshopper. A sticky tongue and swiveling eyes aid the hunter. Madagascar's chameleons can produce rainbows of changing colors.

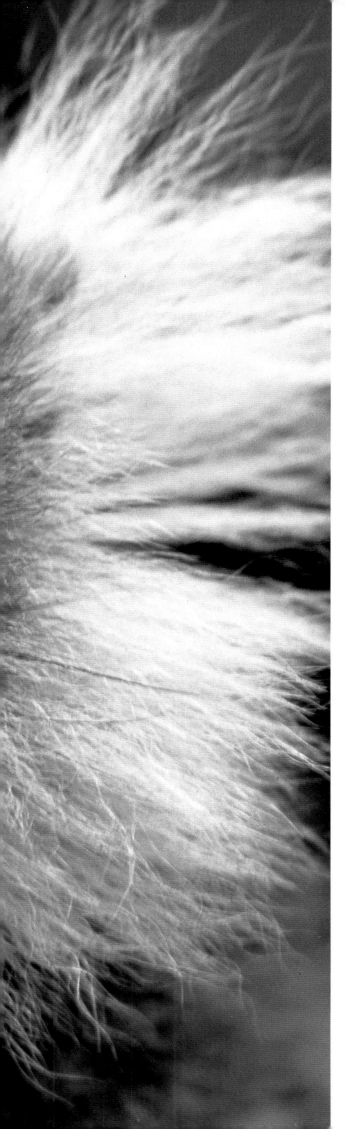

Tree-dwelling brown lemurs (above) make a rare descent to quench their thirst. The scent of a fossa—a feared predator—lingers, making them nervous. Traveling in trees, the lemur moves on all fours, using its long tail for balance.

Female black lemurs like this one (opposite) are believed to be leaders of troops that rush around treetops, keeping in touch with calls for greetings, threats, and alarms. Births seem to coincide with the start of the rainy season, the best time for a lemur to begin life.

With a baby clutching her back, a sifaka (above) leaps between trees. Propelled by powerful legs, sifakas can leap about 30 feet. On the ground, they move about by hopping, arms extended for balance.

Sifakas cluster in a tree (opposite), part of their high-level homeland. Traveling as a troop from tree to tree, sifakas claim an arboreal territory, which they harvest for fruits and flowers in rainy seasons and for leaves in dry times.

SEEING WILDLIFE

VISITORS who want to see African wildlife usually seek "The Big Five"—lion, elephant, leopard, rhino and buffalo. The best chance of seeing most of The Big Five is on the Serengeti, part of Tanzania's central plateau and the site of Serengeti National Park /Ngorongoro Conservation Area. Here visitors will also see wildebeests, gazelles, hyenas, cheetahs, zebras, hippopotamuses, giraffes, elephants, and rhinoceroses.

About 11 percent of Tanzania is dedicated to national parks and game reserves. Zambia has made a similar commitment, allocating about one-third of its area to national parks and game management sites.

Namibia's leading wildlife area is Etosha National Park, where elephants, antelope, and black rhinos are on view. More than 600 of the 903 bird species of southern Africa live in Namibia

In Botswana's Chobe National Park there are more than 460 species of birds; the park supports one of Africa's largest known elephant populations. The Okavango Delta, west of Chobe, is the world's largest inland delta and includes the Moremi Wildlife Reserve. Access is from Maun or Mekoro. Most people are flown in by concessionaires. Only the eastern portion of Moremi is open to the public. Animals include lions, leopards, wild dogs, servals, elephants, hippos, various antelope, and buffalo.

One of South Africa's finest parks is Kruger National Park, where all The Big Five can be found, along with wild dogs, cheetahs, hyenas, impalas, hippos, crocodiles, and spectacular bird life. Skukuza (park headquarters, in the south) is 310 miles by tar road from Johannesburg.

The parks cited above are among those numbered on the map (opposite). Selected with the aid of the World Wildlife Fund, they are among Africa's premier sites for viewing wildlife.

1. Masai Mara National Reserve, Kenya
2. Nakuru National Park, Kenya
3. Samburu National Reserve, Kenya
4. Amboseli National Park, Kenya
5. Tsavo East and West National Park, Kenya
6. Serengeti National Park/Ngorongoro Conservation Area, Tanzania
7. Lake Manyara National Park, Tanzania
8. Tarangire National Park, Tanzania
9. Selous Game Reserve, Tanzania
10. Queen Elizabeth National Park, Uganda
11. Kibale Forest National Park, Uganda
12. Murchison Falls National Park, Uganda
13. Bwindi National Park, Uganda
14. Virunga National Park, Zaire
15. Volcanoes National Park, Rwanda
16. South Luangwa National Park, Zambia
17. Hwange National Park, Zimbabwe
18. Matusadona National Park, Zimbabwe
19. Mana Pools National Park, Zimbabwe
20. Kruger National Park, South Africa
21. Chobe National Park, Botswana
22. Moremi Wildlife Reserve (Okavango Delta), Botswana
23. Central Kalahari Game Preserve, Botswana
24. Gemsbok National Park, Botswana
25. Namib-Naukluft Park, Namibia
26. Skeleton Coast Park, Namibia
27. Etosha National Park, Namibia
28. Nouabalé-Ndoki National Park, Congo
29. Dzanga-Ndoki National Park/ Dzanga-Sangha Dense Forest Reserve, Central African Republic
30. Waza National Park, Cameroon
31. Nazinga Game Ranch, Burkina Faso
32. Niokolo-Koba National Park, Senegal
33. Amber Mountain National Park/ Ankarana Special Reserve, Madagascar
34. Ranomafana National Park, Madagascar

AFRICA

CAIRO

Nile River

DAKAR

③②

③①

③⓪

Lake Turkana

②⑨ ②⑧

⑫

Lake Victoria

⑪

⑭ ⑩

① ② ③

NAIROBI

⑬

⑥ ④ ⑤

⑮

⑦

⑧

Lake Tanganyika

⑨

Lake Malawi

③③

⑯ ⑲

②⑦

⑱

②⑥

②① ②②

⑰

MADAGASCAR

②③

②⓪

③④

②⑤

②④

CAPE TOWN

ENDANGERED SPECIES

MAMMALS

Tenrecs: 7 species V, E, C
Otter shrews: 3 species E
Golden moles: 11 species V, E, C
Shrews: 62 species V, E, C
Bats: 43 species V, E, C
Pygmy mouse lemur V
Coquerel's dwarf lemur V
Hairy-eared dwarf lemur C
> Fork-marked lemur:
   3 subspecies V[1]
Gray-backed sportive lemur V
Northern sportive lemur V
> Western gentle lemur V
> Alaotran gentle lemur V
Golden bamboo lemur C
Broad-nosed gentle lemur C
Ring-tailed lemur V
> Sanford's lemur V
> White-collared lemur E
> Collared lemur V
Black lemur V
^ Sclater's lemur C[2]
Crowned lemur V
Red-bellied lemur V
Mongoose lemur V
Ruffed lemur E
^ Red-ruffed lemur C
Avahi V
Verreaux's sifaka V
^ Coquerel's sifaka E
^ Crowned sifaka C
Golden-crowned sifaka C
Diademed sifaka E
^ Silky sifaka C
^ Perrier's sifaka C
Indri E
Aye-aye E
Diana monkey V
^ Roloway monkey E
White-throated monkey V
Red-eared guenon V
^ Fernando Po red-eared monkey E
> Kahuzi owl-faced monkey V
> Golden monkey C
> Fernando Po crowned monkey V
Preuss's monkey E
Sclater's guenon E
Sun-tailed monkey V
> White-collared mangabey E
> Sanje mangabey E
> Tana River mangabey E
> Ruwenzori black-and-white
   colobus V
Black colobus V
White-thighed black-and-white
   colobus V
> Bouvier's red colobus E
> Niger Delta red colobus E
> Uehe red colobus E
> Zanzibar red colobus E
> Pennant's red colobus E
> Preuss's red colobus E
> Tana River red colobus E
> Temminck's red colobus E
> Miss Waldron's bay colobus C
Barbary macaque V (north only)
Drill E
Gorilla E
^ Mountain gorilla C

Pygmy chimpanzee E
Chimpanzee E
Ethiopian wolf C
African wild dog E
Crested genet E
Malagasy civet V
Falanouc E
Broad-striped mongoose V
Giant-striped mongoose E
Narrow-striped mongoose V
Brown-tailed mongoose V
Liberian mongoose E
> Sokoke bushy-tailed mongoose E
Jackson's mongoose V
Fossa V
> North African serval E
> North African leopard C
Lion V
Cheetah V
^ Northwest African cheetah E
Mediterranean monk seal C
Dugong V
African manatee V
African elephant E
African wild ass C
Grevy's zebra E
Mountain zebra E
Black rhinoceros C
> Northern white rhinoceros C
Eastern tree hyrax V
Algerian yellow-spotted hyrax V
   (north only)
Zaire yellow-spotted hyrax V
> Western forest hog V
> Somali warthog V
> Eritrean warthog V
> Lake Chad hippopotamus V
Pygmy hippopotamus V
^ Nigerian pygmy hippopotamus C
Mountain nyala V
> Eastern bongo E
> Western giant eland E
Abbott's duiker V
Aders' duiker V
Jentink's duiker V
Zebra duiker V
> Kafue lechwe V
> Black lechwe V
> Western mountain reedbuck E
> Giant sable antelope C
Scimitar-horned oryx C
Addax E
Hunter's antelope C
> Bontebok V
> Korrigum V
> Swayne's hartebeest E
> Tora hartebeest E
> Western klipspringer E
> Haggard's oribi V
Silver dikdik V
Beira antelope V
> Black-faced impala V
Dibatag V
Cuvier's gazelle E (north only)
Dama gazelle E
> Pelzeln's gazelle V
Red-fronted gazelle V
Slender-horned gazelle E
Soemmerring's gazelle V
Speke's gazelle V

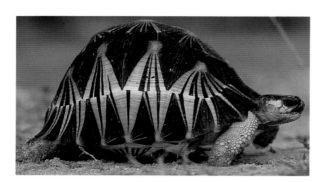

*The geometric tortoise is one of eight
endangered African tortoise species.*

THE AFRICAN species and subspecies on this page are classified as critically endangered (C), endangered (E), or vulnerable (V) in the *1996 IUCN Red List of Threatened Animals*, published by the International Union for Conservation of Nature and Natural Resources. Some animals, such as gorillas, have a full species classification, with a more serious classification for subspecies.

The list does not include whales, dolphins, or fish; 118 fresh-water species are endangered, as is the coelacanth, an ancient fish once thought extinct. There are also 235 African invertebrates on the list of threatened animals.

The area included encompasses Madagascar and Comoros (as indicated); Sao Tome and Fernando Po islands. Not included are animals endangered in the Seychelles or other islands in Indian Ocean; the Canaries or other islands off the northwest coast of Africa. Species found only north of Sahara are indicated by "north only." Some groups of related species are combined, as indicated.

Nubian ibex E
Walia ibex C
Barbary sheep V (north only)
Squirrels: 5 species V
Rats and Mice: 36 species V, E, C
Gerbils: 15 species V, E, C
Springhare V
Felou gundi V
South African dormouse V
Riverine rabbit E
Elephant shrews: 7 species V, E

BIRDS
Madagascar grebe V
Alaotra grebe C
Wandering albatross V
Dalmatian pelican V (north only)
Madagascar heron V
Slaty egret V
Dwarf olive ibis C

Southern bald ibis V
Northern bald ibis C
Madagascar teal E
Madagascar pochard C
Ferruginous duck V
Marbled teal V (north only)
White-headed duck V (north only)
Spanish imperial eagle V
   (north only)
Greater spotted eagle V (north only)
Imperial eagle V
Madagascar serpent eagle C
Cape griffon V
Madagascar fish-eagle C
Taita falcon V
Lesser kestrel V
Congo peafowl V
White-breasted guineafowl V
Francolins: 5 species V, C
Udzungwa forest-partridge E

Mesites: 3 species V
Wattled crane V
Blue crane V
Sakalava rail C
Corncrake V
White-winged flufftail E
Slender-billed flufftail E
Madagascar plover V
Sociable lapwing V
Slender-billed curlew C (north only)
White-eyed gull V
Somali pigeon V
Maroon pigeon V
Black-cheeked lovebird E
Bannerman's turaco V
Prince Ruspoli's turaco E
Congo bay-owl V
Madagascar red owl E
Usambara eagle-owl V
Albertine owlet V
Anjouan scops-owl C
   (Comoros only)
Sokoke scops-owl V
Grand Comoro scops-owl C
   (Comoros only)
Rufous fishing-owl E
Itombwe nightjar V
Schouteden's swift V
Ground-rollers: 4 species V
White-chested tinkerbird V
Yellow-footed honeyguide V
African green broadbill V
Yellow-bellied asity E
Red lark V
Archer's lark E
Rudd's lark C
Sidamo lark E
Ash's lark E
Degodi lark V
Botha's lark V
Blue swallow V
White-tailed swallow V
Red Sea swallow V
Yellow-breasted pipit V
Sokoke pipit V
Western wattled cuckoo-shrike V
Green-tailed bristlebill V
Greenbuls: 6 species V, C, E
Shrikes: 11 species E, C, V
Vangas: 3 species V
Thyolo alethe V
Sao Tome short-tail V
Apalis: 5 species V, C
Dappled mountain-robin V
Black-capped rufous warbler V
Grauer's swamp warbler V
Papyrus yellow warbler V
White-headed robin-chat V
Madagascar yellowbrow V
Turner's eremomela V
Grand Comoro flycatcher V
   (Comoros only)
White-throated mountain-babbler V
Pulitzer's longbill E
Nimba flycatcher V
Chapin's flycatcher V
Red-tailed newtonia V
Long-billed tailorbird C
White-necked rockfowl V
Gray-necked rockfowl V

Banded wattle-eye V
White-eyed prinia V
Benson's rock-thrush V
Mrs. Moreau's warbler V
Akelats: 4 species E, V
Swynnerton's robin V
Annobon paradise flycatcher V
Hinde's pied-babbler E
Taita thrush C
Somali thrush E
Spotted ground-thrush E
Algerian nuthatch E (north only)
Sunbirds 5 species V
Fernado Po speirops V
Principe speirops V
Mount Cameroon speirops V
White-eyes: 6 species V, C
Warsangli linnet E
Sao Tome grosbeak C
Ankober serin E
Yellow-throated serin E
Salvadori's serin V
Shelley's crimson-wing V
Black-lored waxbill V
Anambra waxbill V
Weavers: 12 species V, E, C
Abbott's starling V
Sao Tome oriole V
Grand Comoro drongo C
   (Comoros only)
Mayotte drongo C (Comoros only)
Ethiopian bush-crow V

REPTILES
West African dwarf crocodile V
Chameleons: 6 species V, E, C
Girdled lizards: 5 species V
Geckos: 2 species V
Skinks: 4 species V
Snakes: 6 species V
Green Sea Turtle E
Hawksbill sea turtle C
Olive ridley sea turtle E
Leatherback sea turtle E
Madagascar big-headed turtle E
Turkana mud turtle V
Tortoises: 8 species V, E

AMPHIBIANS
Amatola toad V
Mt. Nimba viviparous toad E
Hewitt's ghost frog E
Table Mountain ghost frog V
Pickersgill's reed frog V
Long-toed tree frog V
Cape rain frog V
Desert rain frog V
Madagascar rain frog V
Cape platanna frog V
Goliath frog V
Madagascar mantella frog V
Micro frog E

---

[1] > in front of a name means that
entry is a subspecies of a species
that is not otherwise listed.

[2] ^ before a name means that the
entry is a subspecies of the
previously listed species.

Index

Much of the basic information on the mammals in this book came from

the authoritative *Walker's Mammals of the World*, whose author, Ronald

M. Nowak, an old and cherished friend, reviewed this book. The author

also wishes to acknowledge the National Geographic Society's

The Marvels of Animal Behavior and *Animals of East Africa* by

Louis S. B. Leakey; Mitsuaki Iwago's *In the Lion's Den*,

John Karmali's *Birds of Africa*, Ken Preston-Mafham's

Madagascar, A Natural History, and Frans Lanting's

Okavango, Africa's Last Eden.